D1544459

STARTING WITH SARTRE

Continuum's *Starting with . . .* series offers clear, concise and accessible introductions to the key thinkers in philosophy. The books explore and illuminate the roots of each philosopher's work and ideas, leading readers to a thorough understanding of the key influences and philosophical foundations from which his or her thought developed. Ideal for first-year students starting out in philosophy, the series will serve as the ideal companion to study of this fascinating subject.

Available now:

Starting with Berkeley, Nick Jones

Starting with Derrida, Sean Gaston

Starting with Descartes, C. G. Prado

Starting with Hegel, Craig B. Matarrese

Starting with Heidegger, Tom Greaves

Starting with Hobbes, George MacDonald Ross

Starting with Nietzsche, Ullrich Haase

Starting with Rousseau, James Delaney

Forthcoming:

Starting with Hume, Charlotte R. Brown and William Edward Morris

Starting with Kant, Andrew Ward

Starting with Kierkegaard, Patrick Sheil

Starting with Leibniz, Lloyd Strickland

Starting with Locke, Greg Forster

Starting with Merleau-Ponty, Katherine Morris

Starting with Mill, John R. Fitzpatrick

Starting with Schopenhauer, Sandra Shapshay

Starting with Wittgenstein, Chon Tejedor

STARTING WITH SARTRE

GAIL LINSENBARD

continuum

Continuum International Publishing Group
The Tower Building   80 Maiden Lane
11 York Road   Suite 704
London SE1 7NX   New York, NY 10038

www.continuumbooks.com

British Library Cataloguing-in-Publication Data
A catalogue record for this book is available from the British Library.

ISBN: HB: 978–1–8470–6527–8
PB: 978–1–8470–6528–5

Library of Congress Cataloging-in-Publication Data
Linsenbard, Gail Evelyn.
Starting with Sartre / Gail Linsenbard.
p. cm.
Includes bibliographical references and index.
ISBN-13: 978–1–84706–527–8 (HB)
ISBN-10: 1–84706–527–9 (HB)
ISBN-13: 978–1–84706–528–5 (pbk.)
ISBN-10: 1–84706–528–7 (pbk.)
1. Sartre, Jean-Paul, 1905–1980.   I. Title.

B2430.S34L56 2010
194–dc22

2009047102

Typeset by RefineCatch Limited, Bungay, Suffolk
Printed and bound in Great Britain by
The MPG Books Group

CONTENTS

ACKNOWLEDGEMENTS

I extend my heartfelt thanks to those who generously helped me in thinking through both the approach and structure of this book. In particular, I would like to thank my students, who continue to remind me of the importance of making philosophy both accessible to a wider public and relevant to the world in which we live. Philosophical discussions with my colleagues, especially of note, Phil Washburn and Michael Shenefelt, were enormously beneficial in working out some of the finer points of analysis. Needless to say, I alone am responsible for any defects or errors in my presentation.

I would also like to thank NYU's Liberal Studies Program for awarding me a Faculty Research Development Grant during the fall 2008 term which gave me valuable time to work on this project.

Finally, I want to thank my mother, Avalin, whose generosity of spirit and unconditional love has sustained me, especially during moments of my deepest doubt.

CHAPTER 1

INTRODUCTION

What I like about my madness is that it has protected me from the very beginning against the charms of the "elite": never have I thought that I was the happy possessor of a "talent"; my sole concern has been to save myself—nothing in my hands, nothing up my sleeve—by work and faith. As a result, my pure choice did not raise me above anyone. Without equipment, without tools, I set all of me to work in order to save all of me. If I relegate impossible Salvation to the prop room, what remains? A whole man, composed of all men and as good as all of them and no better than any.

(Sartre 1964: 255)

Sartre wrote this in 1964 in *The Words*, his autobiography, a work for which he was awarded, but refused, the Nobel Prize in literature. It is instructive to reflect on his passage in relation to Socrates' opening sentence in Plato's *Republic*:

I went down to the Piraeus yesterday with Glaucon, son of Ariston, to pray to the goddess; and, at the same time I wanted to observe how they would put on a festival, since they were now holding it for the first time. (327a)

Nickolas Pappas, Plato scholar and commentator, has noted that in Greek 'I went down' is rendered in a single word, *kateben*, the first word of the *Republic*. This expression, he observes, is especially meaningful because it shows Plato's intention to wrestle with the problem of justice directly and squarely. The expression suggests that Socrates will descend from the heights of his intellectual plane to discuss justice with others, one on one. Throughout the *Republic* Socrates is confronted with the problem of how a perfect or ideal city could emerge from such an imperfect world, and Plato has Socrates 'come down' into the city streets to discuss the problem, rather than discuss it, as he does other topics, in the Agora. Notably, 'Piraeus' was a port city, so one would find not only fisherman, and merchants, but also plenty of itinerant traders, foreigners and, of course, criminals. 'I went down' also anticipates Book 7 in the *Republic*, where Plato offers the 'Allegory of the Cave', portraying prisoners in everyday life shackled and blindsided by ignorance and fear in a cave of shadows and images. Socrates contrasts this kind of existence with the life of the philosopher who is able to look beyond the shadows on the long and arduous path of enlightenment and discover the brightly lit reality of the world outside of the cave. The philosopher, we are told, must return to the cave to help the others see what she has seen.

As a philosopher Sartre felt the need to descend from his intellectual heights and offer his philosophy to living, experiencing human beings who feel vulnerable in an increasingly fractured world. He did not raise himself above the world or, indeed, above anyone. He loathed what today we might call 'armchair' philosophy, a practice that has all too often given philosophy the deserved reputation it has, namely, that it is, or ought to be, removed from the everyday concerns of individuals, reserved only for the intellectual 'elite' who have proven themselves particularly adept in abstract conceptual analysis, logical erudition and rigorous debate. Although Sartre also expressed his philosophical ideas in dauntingly technical and dense language, especially so in his major philosophical work, *Being and Nothingness*, that made it virtually inaccessible to non-specialists, he nonetheless brought existentialism, the philosophical movement for which he became famous, 'home' to the public through his fiction, biography, plays, literary criticism and journalism.

Like the American pragmatist, William James (1842–1910), a philosopher whom he read, Sartre believed that philosophy should endeavour to change people's lives for the better, and he was committed to the view that not only philosophers, but all of us, should strive to ameliorate human suffering and social injustice. With James, he wanted philosophy to be accessible and genuinely felt by as many people as possible. Sartre was catapulted to fame after his attempt to popularize existentialism in his 'speech' on 'the humanism' of existentialism, given in Paris in 1946; his lecture was attended by so many people that there were reports of people fainting, and a near stampede. In all of Sartre's works, and certainly most clearly dramatized in his fiction and plays, there is a constant undercurrent of morally charged issues and problems hanging in the balance – always punctuated by choices that must be made, and our 'human, all to human' effort to avoid making them, to evade them or, alternatively, to take responsibility for them. He emphasizes again and again that we are fundamentally free to make and re-make our lives, notwithstanding the real and often recalcitrant obstacles, including especially other people, who inevitably stand in our way. And however we choose to 'make ourselves', we always do so in the midst of others, he noted, because we live in a 'peopled world' where, as Simone de Beauvoir, a philosopher in her own right and Sartre's lifelong companion observes, 'the other is my concern'. Sartre was ever mindful of finding ways, through our freely chosen creative endeavours, to improve the lives of others; he despised complacency as much as he hated social injustice and attempts to hide, ignore or silence the lived experiences of persons. For Sartre, as we will appreciate in subsequent chapters, the need to relieve suffering and remedy injustice by attending to the real needs of people and by promoting rather than 'stealing' their freedom from them, was always front and centre from the beginning to the end of his career.

Throughout his life Sartre eloquently and passionately defended the individual against what he took to be a tendency in philosophy to reduce or ignore human experiences. We might say, then, that Sartre's chief concern is to grasp the truth of the lived experiences of people as they grapple with brute, inexorable obstacles in the presence of others who are both for and against them, and to freely make choices in a world where economic, social, political and cultural structures that have served to thwart rather than enhance flourishing, have become entrenched. How do we not merely survive, but also thrive and flourish in a contingent world with real possibilities and real dangers? It is up to all of us, Sartre believed, to answer these questions and moreover, offer viable solutions to the world's problems. As we will see, on Sartre's view, no one is relieved from the responsibility of making choices while they are here; it is only after our death that the burden of making choices ceases, at which time the sum total of our choices will be left behind – the only 'mark' on the world that is uniquely ours and that will remain for others to take up or ignore after we are gone.

There is, then, a distinctive kind of humanism driving Sartre's philosophical outlook. This humanism both motivates and unifies his writings and, while we are only concerned to explore Sartre's early philosophy and the philosophical predecessors who most influenced him, we may note here that Sartre's humanism serves to bridge any supposed gap that might be said to exist between the 'early' and 'later' Sartre. Rejecting a transcendent God or prior structure/order that could underwrite values in the world, Sartre locates the source of values in us, and in so doing opens up a range of possibilities that could, through our choosing them, become real. Hence, Sartre is timeless in the sense that 'the moral problem' is a human problem that confronts us directly. It will be up to us to decide what values we will inscribe into the universe that will offer possibilities for altering the configuration of the world today: the possibility of eliminating the ever widening gap between the wealthy and the poor; the possibility of ameliorating suffering caused by the insensitive and cruel choices of others; the possibility of reducing the pernicious effects of climate change; the possibility of changing human practices to protect an increasingly fragile planet; the possibility to live in peace; the possibility to create the conditions for authentic love, care, and compassion; the possibility to integrate joy into our daily lives by eliminating material deprivation and fulfilling fundamental needs; in short, the possibility to live genuine human lives where the Other is the concern of each one of us.

Let us turn, then, to the business of understanding Sartre, both by himself and through the inspiration of some of his more inspiring predecessors, to wit, Socrates, Descartes, Kant, Husserl and Heidegger. We shall begin with philosophy's most venerated practitioner, Socrates, the 'gadfly' of philosophy. Starting with Socrates will prove especially edifying because, as we will see, Socrates, too, wanted to 'bring philosophy home' to a world of experiencing, living and feeling creatures; he would have thus applauded Sartre's lifelong commitment to challenge the status quo and bring about a world in which we do not *merely* exist, but are able to live in joy, abundance and love.

CHAPTER 2

SOCRATIC INSPIRATIONS

In reality, seeking is seeking, that is, it implies the permanent risk of not finding, of dying without having found. To say that I have found is to make myself into God's puppet.

(Sartre 1992: 326)

i. THE TASK OF PHILOSOPHY

It is difficult to find in the history of ideas a philosopher who expressed more sympathy, humanity and outrage at the world's injustices than did Jean-Paul Sartre. *Starting with Sartre* is thus to engage one of the most provocative, controversial and committed thinkers of the twentieth century. No less than Socrates, western philosophy's most celebrated thinker, the task of philosophy for Sartre is to reach concretely existing people on the street, to speak to them directly, to awaken them and encourage them to think more deeply and critically; in essence, the task of philosophy is to stir and prod a complacent public to live as though there were no tomorrow. Sartre wanted, as James expressed it, philosophy to be 'brought home' to living, experiencing human beings who live in a world that is often dangerous and uncertain. Indeed, this is why, in addition to formal philosophical writing, Sartre elaborated his philosophical views in multiple genres, including fiction, plays and biography. The wider audience he could reach, the more universally his philosophy might resonate and be applied to real world problems and concerns.

Throughout his life Sartre eloquently and passionately defended the individual against what he took to be a tendency in formal philosophy and science to reduce or ignore the concrete, lived human experiences of persons. In this respect his concern is reminiscent of the nineteenth-century Danish philosopher, Søren Kierkegaard (1813–1855), who passionately defended the individual against the broader tendency in philosophy, most strongly expressed in the philosophy of Hegel (1770–1831), the nineteenth-century German philosophical giant, to bury the individual in the folds of abstract ideas, or in a grander, abstruse philosophical system that encompassed the whole of history. In our own century, Sartre would have found the tendency in neuroscience not so much to bury or hide the individual, but to reduce human experiences to the biochemical structure or processes in the brain as equally misguided. Questions, for example, that typically appear in popular magazines, to wit, 'Are we our Genes?' and 'Is Belief in God Hard-wired?, underscore this tendency. This is not to say that Sartre ignores or lacks respect for the biological sciences, but rather that he regarded the attempt of *any* discipline to tell the whole story or have the final word concerning the ultimate or true meaning of our human experiences as pretentious and wrong-headed. The discipline of science rightly commands our respect and, ever since the scientific revolution in the seventeenth century, science has been making such great strides that it now outranks other disciplines as the most revered in the academy. Philosophy, a discipline that historically encompassed science, has been trying to catch up ever since, but it increasingly finds itself trailing far behind the sciences in terms of respectability and worthiness of inquiry. And past as well as more recent attempts in philosophy to become more scientific have tended to dismiss as irrelevant other approaches and methods of philosophical inquiry that may well be worthy of our attention.

As a phenomenologist and ontologist, Sartre's approach and method in philosophical inquiry is to describe our *lived* human experiences and what it means to exist as a human being. Sartre was first introduced to phenomenology through the writings of the founder of the phenomenological movement, the Czech-German philosopher Edmund Husserl (1859–1938), whose influence on him was both profound and lasting. Sartre's lifelong companion, the French philosopher de Beauvoir (1908–1985), relates how Sartre first became acquainted with phenomenology while they were enjoying apricot cocktails at a Paris café with their friend and, for a time, fellow-intellectual traveller, Raymond Aron. de Beauvoir tells how Aron announced, as he pointed to his glass, 'You see my dear fellow, if you are a phenomenologist, you can talk about this cocktail and make philosophy out of it!' de Beauvoir tells us that 'Sartre turned pale with emotion at this. Here was just the thing he had been longing to achieve for years – to describe objects just as he saw and touched them, and extract philosophy from the process' (de Beauvoir 1966: 162). Sartre then rushed to a bookstore to find Husserl's text, quickly devoured it, and made arrangements to travel to Germany for one year to study phenomenology and to be where all the excitement was. We will speak in Chapter 4 in greater detail about phenomenology, but briefly note here that the aim of phenomenology is to offer a descriptive account of the objects of our experience, or phenomena, as they appear to consciousness and, of no less importance, of the essential structures of conscious activity itself. The deep attraction the study of phenomenology had for Sartre was that it seemed to suggest that we could directly grasp the objects of our experience, and that there was a strict correlation between our conscious awareness and the objects of our conscious awareness. Phenomenology also held the promise of realism, a doctrine to which Sartre was wholeheartedly committed, because it implied that the world of which we are conscious is just the world as it is, without veils of appearances clouding our experiences. Husserl's slogan, 'To the things themselves!' can be readily appreciated here; we need not worry about a deeper reality under the one we experience since, Husserl notes, phenomenological method will suspend or 'bracket' questions concerning the real existence of entities or objects, and focus solely on their appearance to consciousness.

Of critical importance under the influence of one of Husserl's pupils, the German philosopher Martin Heidegger (1889–1976), Sartre insists, over against Husserl, that a phenomenological study must be carried out in conjunction with an ontological investigation, which is the study of the fundamental kinds of being that exist in the world: what are the most basic things that exist in the world and constitute 'reality'? For Sartre, phenomenology and ontology perform a kind of 'marriage function' in that the descriptive study of the essential structures of consciousness is always carried out against a world of objects and subjects of which one is conscious: we describe the world of our experience exactly as we experience it. It is not proper phenomenological procedure, then, to sacrifice consciousness to a world of mere things, any more than it is proper to reject or dismiss the reality of things as mere ideas in our conscious awareness; one of Sartre's signature contributions to philosophy is that he rejects both of these reductive tendencies.

As a phenomenologist and ontologist, then, one of Sartre's most pressing questions concerned the proper description of our unique human way of existing. The first order of business, he believed, must be to offer an account of what it means to exist as a human being; any other inquiries, he held, including scientific ones, would have to take account of the fundamental findings of a phenomenological investigation – unless they do not concern human affairs. Among Sartre's findings is that persons are free to make and remake themselves in a world that offers resistance. Thus in addition to finding strictly reductionist neuro-scientific accounts of human action unsatisfactory because, among other things, they deny the experience of human freedom, Sartre would have also found the tendency among Anglo-American analytic philosophers to adopt a determinist account of human behaviour that denies the experience of human freedom as indefensible.[1] As a staunch defender of human freedom, Sartre convincingly argues that freedom is experienced directly, and his principal philosophical interest is to defend the reality of human freedom against its detractors and to understand and sympathize with the *lived experiences* of persons. A key component of this interest, as we shall see, is to inspire persons to live their lives in ways that would freely and creatively inscribe values in the world. At the top of his list of values that he thought were most worthy of our attention was generosity because it is through generosity that we may most effectively increase human flourishing and reduce suffering caused by oppression.

While Socrates and Sartre did not share a philosophical method and while there are important points of divergence between them, it is nonetheless striking the extent to which both philosophers had in common regarding the task of philosophy. With Socrates (and, indeed, James too), Sartre emphasizes philosophy as *doing* and *practice* – as a way of *living*; he is deeply committed to the view that the value of philosophy lies in the real, felt and practical difference it can make to the actual lives of persons. In his *Humanism* lecture, for example, Sartre dramatically declares, 'Man is a project which possesses a subjective life, instead of being a kind of moss, or a fungus or a cauliflower'; in this same lecture he states unequivocally, 'our point of departure is the subjectivity of the individual'. Both

Socrates and Sartre understand and defend philosophy as a distinct-ive kind of humanism because philosophy asks the most pressing human questions and addresses the most fundamental human issues, to wit, the meaning of life, the questions of human freedom and moral responsibility and the inevitability of every person's death. For both philosophers the task of philosophy is austere and joyful; it reveals to us our most human possibilities and our greatest fears, and asks us to confront our deepest and gravest challenges with abiding courage and conviction.

ii. THE PHILOSOPHER AS GADFLY

If, indeed, the aim of philosophy is, as Socrates tells us, to 'Know Thyself' and to remind us throughout our lives that 'the unexamined life is not worth living', then Sartre stands alongside Socrates as a philosopher who insists that our ideals must be actively and pas-sionately lived, not merely held or thought in the abstract. Similar to the Socratic dictum to 'Know Thyself', Sartre's pronouncements that we 'are condemned to be free' and 'have the life we deserve' emphasize a kind of deep responsibility that presupposes the free-dom to which he was committed throughout his life. With these claims Sartre stresses that our lives are the sum total of the choices we have freely made and, to the extent that we have refrained from creating values that allow our humanity to genuinely flourish, we deserve the life that we have, since we could have always chosen differently; hence, he insists, our responsibility for the kind of life we have is much greater than we might have supposed.

While Socrates does not really speak of freedom at all, not to mention freedom as 'total', 'complete' and 'absolute' in Sartre's sense, he does speak of wilful ignorance and culpable indifference to the ways in which our acts and omissions bear on the lives of others and on the world in which we live. And it is in this sense that Socrates may be considered the earliest existentialist: his stubborn questioning of both himself and others (to wit: What is justice? What is courage? What is piety? What is love? What is wisdom?), and his relentless search for truth point to his commitment that the task of philosophy is to inquire into the meaning of our existence and our reasons for living one way as opposed to another way. These, of course, are deeply existential questions because they go to the heart of our humanity: they ask us to reflect on our uniquely human way of existing. They are also among the most important questions we can ask about ourselves, our relations to others, and to the world in which we live. Hence the Socratic dicta to 'Know Thyself' and 'The unexamined life is not worth living' are existential in a Sartrean sense in that they urge us to reject ignorance, apathy and indifference and ask us to be attentive to the impact our actions and omissions have on others and the world. For both Sartre and Socrates, our philosophical task is to accept the challenge to discover (for Socrates) or face up to (for Sartre) the truth about ourselves and our relations with others; for both philosophers, discovering this 'truth' will involve a commitment to living our lives with the kind of critical self-awareness and questioning that contests the meaning we already find in the world, and accepting the responsibility of forging values that more closely reflect our deepest ideals. For Socrates such ideals would surely include our commitment to Truth itself – that is, to committing oneself to the discovery of Truth through the careful analysis of language and the meaning of concepts and terms we use to express virtues such as justice, courage and wisdom. To be sure, Socrates was deeply committed to the view that truth exists, that it is worth pursuing, and that the 'good life' involves our active, ongoing pursuit of it. Sartre, too, is concerned with discovering truth, but unlike Socrates, such a discovery was not a strictly rational pursuit. As a phenomenologist, Sartre did not privilege thinking or reason, as Socrates did; Sartre's phenomenological pursuit of truth, as we have seen, involves the human ability to describe both the activity of experiencing that of which we are consciously aware and the object of that experience itself. As we have also noted, Sartre argued that among the many things we experience, we experience ourselves as free. It also seems to be true, he observed, that for the most part we do not want to accept the reality of our freedom because it is far too anxiety provoking, so we tend to make excuses or offer reasons for why we believe we are not free. Indeed, this is why Sartre insists that it is in anguish that we experience ourselves as free. Thus facing up to the truth of our freedom became for Sartre an overriding concern that preoccupied him throughout his life in his numerous philosophical, literary, biographical and political writings.

The ever-present tendency to lie to ourselves about the issue of our freedom is ubiquitous in the human condition and what Sartre calls 'bad faith', a phenomenon about which we will say much more about later. For now it is important to point out that, on Sartre's account, it is difficult to overcome because we tend to exploit the chasm between knowing and not knowing, between knowledge, which can never be absolutely certain or complete, and ignorance. Socrates, of course, knew only too well of the human tendency to look the other way in the face of uncomfortable truths and, like Sartre, he attributes this tendency to the 'human all too human' failure to authentically confront the exigencies of our existence. To be sure, Socrates' unpopularity in the streets of Athens was due in part to his habit of relentlessly questioning his fellow Athenians concerning matters about which they claimed a certain expertise, but in reality knew little or nothing about. Once Socrates exposed their careless ignorance, what Sartre would surely call 'bad faith', his interlocutors would leave the inquisition deeply frustrated and often very embarrassed. Socrates desperately wanted to reach truth by arriving, through critical examination known as the dialectic, at the proper definition of evaluative terms (What is justice? What is love? What is piety?); his interlocutors often claimed a noble reputation attached to these terms, but in point of fact their reputation rang hollow when asked for a definition that was inevitably shown by Socrates to be woefully inadequate upon examination. Socrates soon adopted the label of 'gadfly' because of his penchant for attaching himself to his interlocutors as an insect might sting or bite a horse, with the consequence of annoying them to the point of fury. Thus in the dialogue *Euthyphro*, Socrates buttonholes poor Euthyphro and questions him about the meaning of piety, something Euthyphro claims to know about, to the point of exhaustion; frustrated and annoyed, Euthyphro leaves the inquisition without having learned what piety is, on the one hand, but also having learned that what he thought piety was is in fact false. Socrates convincingly demonstrated that most of his fellow Athenians cared little or nothing for truth, or even for approximating truth; he uncovered the very human tendency not only to lie to other people, but to lie to ourselves as well, so willingly do we believe the lies we tell ourselves and so convincingly do we then tell these lies to others with the effect of deceiving them, in turn. As we shall see, Sartre is no less circumspect regarding the lies we tell ourselves and others, and his diagnosis of the human condition is, equally, uncompromisingly austere.

iii. SARTRE'S SOCRATIC SENSIBILITY: REASON VS. LIVED EXPERIENCE

In *Starting with Sartre* we can appreciate that Sartre was strongly Socratic in both temperament and philosophical sensibility. As we have already noted, while it is true that Sartre does not, as does Socrates, champion reason as the best path to enlightenment, he is deeply Socratic in that he was committed to the view that the most important philosophical questions and issues concern how we live our lives in a world that is fraught with uncertainty. With Socrates, Sartre strongly believed that philosophy could change our lives for the better if we took the care and trouble to concern ourselves with critically attuning our lives so we may create values that most effectively allow us to live well; for Sartre this would amount to inscribing values in the world that aim at ameliorating injustice and oppression, the principal causes of human suffering. Both philosophers were extraordinarily passionate about bringing philosophical ideas to the street because both believed that critical awareness and understanding could inform our actions and lives in profound ways that could make our world more humane and just. Indeed, the death of Socrates, as recorded by Plato in the *Phaedo*, is not merely a symbolic gesture of a man grown weary of existence and mechanically carrying out the will of his fellow Athenians. It is, as Sartre reflects in his *Notebooks for an Ethics*, the culmination of a man 'whose consciousness wills to make itself' (Sartre 1992: 91). Socrates represents the constant Sartrean motif of a man willing to make and remake himself in bringing the importance of critical awareness to bear upon the world and its injustices amidst great resistance and difficulty.

To be sure, in philosophical discussions with his fellow Athenians in the agora Socrates always insisted on clarity and precision and, as we have noted, he was especially keen to hammer down the proper definition of moral or evaluative terms such as justice, courage and goodness. Through the lens of Plato, we see that Socrates held that the search for truth must involve the intellect's use of reason over against sensory experience; because our experiences constantly change, he judged that experience is an unreliable guide to truth and could, at best, only yield opinion, but never certainty or knowledge that was worthy of the title. As a phenomenologist, we have seen that Sartre privileges our conscious awareness and lived experience over against rational insight, which he regarded as far too abstract and removed from our lives as they are actually lived. This is not to say, however, that Sartre is wholly unconcerned with the role reason plays in our lives; it is simply to say that for him actions are what are primarily intelligible. As both a phenomenologist and existentialist, the most important philosophical questions for Sartre concern our *existing* as opposed to our knowing or reasoning. But this manifestly does not mean Sartre is unconcerned with reason or knowledge, any more than it means that Socrates is unconcerned with questions about the meaning of human existence. For both philosophers, *what* we claim to know and *how* we know greatly affects how we act: *the unexamined life is not worth living* is a statement that is both Socratic and Sartrean in that what and how we think (and what claim to know) greatly influences how we exist and live, no less than how we exist and live similarly informs and reinforces what and how we think and believe to be true. Thought, and in particular, critical awareness, and action inform one another and mutually impact the *quality* of our lives and the lives of those around us.

We have seen that while Socrates privileges knowing and Sartre privileges action in the search for a meaningful life, neither philosopher so sharply divides knowing from action that there is not considerable overlap and mutual reinforcement. Thus, in *Euthyphro*, when Socrates finds Euthyphro at court preparing to prosecute his father for impiety, we learn that Socrates is concerned both with understanding the true definition of piety and of calling into question the deeper moral problem of Euthyphro prosecuting his own father for impiety. Through persistent questioning, Socrates uncovers the pretension of Euthyphro, a priest, to know everything there is to know about piety, reducing it to the specific act of what he is doing 'here and now', namely, prosecuting his father. And we discover that Socrates is not satisfied with this definition since he is in search of a much broader, more general and universal definition, one that would cover all instances of piety rather than just one particular act serving as a definition. Hence one lesson conveyed in *Euthyphro* is that our assumptions about the definition of moral terms inform our actions and in turn inescapably affect the lives of others; equally, our actions reflect and reinforce our underlying assumptions, beliefs and reasons. Theory and practice, then, or better, knowledge and action are never far apart, and are in fact inextricably linked. Sartre would have applauded Socrates' examination of Euthyphro, particularly in light of the latter's uncritical, casual and superficial account of piety as merely 'prosecuting wrongdoers' since such an account presupposes expertise attached to a particular role or title that Euthyphro did not in point of fact have. Sartre claimed that much of human misery can be explained by our inattention to life's most unsavoury details and our uncritical acceptance of convenient truths, which are really only half-truths or worse, lies. One is reminded here of Al Gore's film *An Inconvenient Truth* that demonstrates how the 'real truth' of global warming, supported by scientific evidence, is portrayed by others with a vested financial interest as a myth or fiction to maintain their wealth and power.

iv. 'HATED CONSCIENCE' OF THEIR TIME

We have seen the sense in which some of Sartre's approach to philosophical questions may be seen in a Socratic light; particularly relevant here is his view that philosophy is a distinctive kind of *practice* that encourages cultivating a critical awareness of ourselves as agents acting in ways that inscribe values in the world that allow us to live better, more examined lives. If starting with Sartre evokes the spirit of Socrates, arguably among the most beloved philosophers the world has ever known (notwithstanding that he was ridiculed, rebuked, tried and sentenced to death by his fellow Athenians), it is notable that Sartre's legacy has been decidedly less positive, his detractors (and there are many) still vocal and vehement after his death in 1980. Indeed, perhaps no other philosopher (besides Socrates) has been both so gravely misunderstood and vilified in the history of ideas. Notably, a good friend of Sartre's, John Gerassi, titled his book on Sartre *Hated Conscience of His Century* to underscore this sentiment. Socrates, we know, did not escape the hatred of his fellow Athenians; Plato's heartfelt account of his trial, defence and dignified death testify to this. It was only after Socrates' death, through the writings of Plato, that Socrates became so beloved; indeed, his legacy became sealed as future generations acknowledged their debt to him as a man who became for them an unparalleled moral exemplar.

Both Socrates and Sartre were misunderstood and hated during their lives because others found their views deeply threatening and, in Sartre's case especially, deeply repugnant. There is nothing more difficult or threatening than to remove the veils of wilful ignorance and self-deception, particularly when the disclosure of truth threatens to undermine vested powerful interests; both Socrates and Sartre were 'gadfly' philosophers who tried relentlessly and tirelessly to awaken a sleeping public. Facing up to uncomfortable truths about ourselves and our humanity is a burdensome task, to be sure, and sometimes depressing; it is so much easier, we think, to simply keep our heads in the sand while convincing ourselves that we are nonetheless alert and awake. Keeping us awake and honest is for both Socrates and Sartre the perennial philosophical challenge – a challenge to which Sartre devoted his entire life and a cause for which Socrates died. In this sense it has been said that 'the existentialist revolt' in philosophy is anything but a rejection of traditional philosophy; in point of fact the recurring existential hero is Socrates and existentialism is, to a large extent, an attempt to return philosophy to its historical foundations (Solomon 1981). The existentialist revolt in philosophy may also be seen in traditional moral philosophy, most notably, as a revolt against the moral views of one of philosophy's giants, Immanuel Kant (1724–1650). We will see in Chapter 7 the extent to which Sartre was keenly interested in Kant's views on morality, especially because he sees the moral implications of his own philosophy as radically opposed to Kant's.

Before we are ready to appreciate Sartre's criticisms of Kant, certainly one of the most influential philosophers in the tradition, we will first pay tribute to those philosophers who greatly influenced Sartre's philosophical development. We begin with the inspiration of a fellow Frenchman, René Descartes (1596–1650), the 'father of modern philosophy'.

CHAPTER 3

THE IMPORTANCE OF DESCARTES

Therefore it can only be through Nothingness that Being resists God. Which is just how Descartes understood things. There must be a continual creation, otherwise the Being of the world would collapse into Nothingness. Nothingness, therefore, is the guarantee of transcendence.

(Sartre 1992: 526)

i. DESCARTES' REVOLUTIONARY SPIRIT

Frenchman that he is, starting with Sartre is also to start with the 'father of modern philosophy', René Descartes. Indeed, it could be argued that Sartre's major philosophical tome, *Being and Nothingness*, is an attempt to work out some of the deepest philosophical problems and issues first raised by Descartes' *Meditations on First Philosophy*. Among these are the problems of perception, the nature of the self (what it means to be self-aware), or the 'cogito' ('I think therefore I am'), and the idea of human freedom.

Descartes is enormously important in the history of ideas because he breaks powerfully with the influence of the Catholic Church in asserting that his own existence as a 'thing that thinks' can be known independently of God. He thereby radically opens a new route for philosophy by wrenching it away from the yoke of theology and showing that philosophical thinking may be, indeed *must* be, carried out independently of theological constraints. Endorsing the Enlightenment dictum, 'Think for yourself', Descartes paves a new way by demonstrating that he is able to think for himself, quite independently of the rules, regulations and dictates of Catholic orthodoxy and authority; he thus claims for himself the independence and power of his own thinking.

Descartes' famous method, the method of systematic doubt, introduces a radical break with the medieval tradition that preceded him in that it introduces a breach between Descartes' sense of himself as a conscious substance on the one hand (Descartes invokes medieval terminological conventions by using such terms as 'substance' by which he means a *non-material* thinking thing), and his knowledge of God and the world outside of him on the other. Medieval philosophers had appealed to God in order to confirm everything that could be known about the self and the outside world; one's own existence and indeed everything else, including knowledge of God, they held, may be known directly through natural reason given to us by God. Importantly, Descartes does not wholly part with this tradition because he is a man of faith and, more urgently, he finds in the course of his analysis that he needs to demonstrate God's existence and goodness before he can proceed to prove the existence of the external world. Thus, in *Meditations* Descartes offers three proofs for God's existence, just in case anyone is inclined to doubt it or is not satisfied with the first two proofs he offers. But Descartes nonetheless makes a radical new start in first proving the existence of *himself* as a thinking thing, independent of God, and with this move we can truly appreciate his revolutionary spirit. Indeed, just as Galileo stunned the Catholic Church with his endorsement of the Copernican view that the earth revolves around the sun and is thus not the centre of the universe, Descartes, although much more cautiously, upended the orthodoxy of the Church in claiming that he could prove his own self-awareness and existence as a thinking thing independently of God.

ii. DESCARTES' STRATEGY

We can best appreciate Descartes' revolutionary attitude, as well as his influence on Sartre, if we review just briefly his strategy, the stages of methodological doubt found in the First Meditation and the one, single truth he is able to arrive at in his Second Meditation, following his stages of doubt.

Insisting on a procedure that provides Descartes with the standards he wants, namely, absolute certainty and clarity of our ideas, Descartes asks us to engage with him in a thought experiment.

Might it be possible, he wonders, for us to doubt everything that presents itself to our minds as objects of perception? That is, in order for us to arrive at knowledge that is clear and distinct, which means that we may have no occasion to doubt it, shouldn't we doubt everything that falls short of absolute certainty *because* it might be doubted? Thus Descartes' strategy is to systematically call into question the veracity of all of the ideas that he has previously held if these ideas lend themselves to even the slightest possibility of doubt. That is, he attempts to make a clean sweep of all previously held beliefs in the hope that he may find just one proposition or one belief that is immune from doubt, and hence known most clearly, most distinctly, and with the utmost certainty. He hopes that he will be able to build or reconstruct upon this foundation all knowledge that is worthy of the name. This is the famous 'Cartesian Method of Doubt'.

The first order of business for Descartes, then, is to doubt the existence of the external world, that is, to doubt those objects of our perception that are at a distance from us. Isn't it very often the case, he asks, that objects that are far away from us and grasped by our senses are mistaken to be *other* than what they truly are? For example, isn't it typically our experience that a tall building standing several miles away from where I am seems much smaller than when I am standing directly next to it, or under it looking up? Thus my initial judgement when seeing the building at a distance for the first time is that the building is in fact not so tall, but I find that this judgement becomes increasingly questionable the closer I get to it; having arrived just a few feet from the building, I judge its true height to be much taller than what I first thought. To take another example, isn't it true that a straight stick floating on the surface of the water seems to be bent because of the effect of the motion of the water on our visual perception? When I retrieve the stick from the water I see that it is not bent, but fairly straight. Once again, then, my senses have been shown to deceive me. Hence, Descartes concludes, the first stage of doubt must be to doubt objects that are far away because his senses have been shown to be unreliable paths to truth. And, he observes, we cannot *ever* trust the senses because we can never be certain when they are deceiving us and when they are not; it is in this sense that, like Socrates and Plato, Descartes is a rationalist who privileges reason over our experience. In just the same way, it would be unwise to trust a friend who has once deceived us because she may very well deceive us again; so Descartes concludes we ought not to trust that the senses will not repeatedly deceive us. At this stage of doubt, the senses have been shown to be unreliable sources of truth with respect to objects at a distance.

What about objects that are close to us? Surely, we seem far less uncertain about objects of our perception that are directly in front of us. Descartes notes, for example, that he can hardly doubt that he is sitting at his desk in his dressing gown, holding his pen between his fingers, and writing on a piece of paper. He feels, he says, the warmth of the fire in the stove; he feels the paper in-between his fingers; he feels himself fully clothed and sitting upright in a chair rather than unclothed in bed. Still, he insists that it is possible to doubt the objects of his perception that are close to him. Why? Because he observes that he may be dreaming that he is sitting in his chair when in fact he is tucked away in his bed. Isn't it at least logically possible, he asks, that we may be dreaming about whatever it is we happen to be doing? Isn't it possible that we may be dreaming that we have a body, but in fact we do not? The mere *possibility* of doubt is enough, Descartes asserts, to call into question our perception that we have a body and that we are physically engaged in a certain task. This is the second stage of doubt Descartes asks us to consider and, while we may readily find challenges to it, our present task is to present it so we may better appreciate Sartre's debt to Descartes, rather than critique it as a philosophical doctrine in its own right. Thus far, then, we have reviewed Descartes' two stages of methodical doubt: we may doubt objects of perception at a distance from us since our senses may be deceiving us, and we may doubt objects of perception close to us, such as our experience of having a body, since it is possible that we may be dreaming we have a body when in fact we do not.

Descartes takes us on one last excursion with respect to the possibility of doubting the objects of our perception. As a mathematician, he much admired the exactness and certainty of geometry and arithmetic. So, he wonders, what about the veracity of mathematical propositions? Surely *they* must be immune from doubt since it is undeniably true that two plus four equals six each and every time I perform the function of addition. But even mathematics, the branch of knowledge that Descartes finds so compelling and certain, can be doubted because, he notes, it is at least logically possible (and anything logically possible is *actually* possible) that every time I add two plus six I am being deceived by an evil genius who, unbeknownst to me, delights in deceiving me at every turn, and especially when I attempt to add two numbers together. So even the heretofore revered and exalted mathematical propositions may be called into question.

Descartes has taken us, finally, to the end of his journey where he has torn asunder the foundations of what he had comfortably called 'his world' as he thought he knew it. He cannot be certain of the existence of the external world because his propositions about it are subject to doubt since that world is known through the senses and the senses have been shown to deceive him. He cannot be certain of the existence of his own body since he is unable to distinguish between what might be a dream and what might be a state of wakefulness. And finally, he cannot be certain of that which he was once most certain, namely, the veracity of mathematical propositions, because he entertains the possibility that he may be systematically deceived by an evil genius every time he adds two plus two, or performs any other mathematical operation. Descartes has now pushed himself into a sceptical corner and it is difficult to see how he might get himself out of it. But wait.

At this juncture, has *anything* escaped Descartes' methodical doubt? Descartes says yes, one thing has, namely his own existence as a thinking thing, which he refers to as the 'I think' or the 'cogito'. Surely, Descartes surmises, it is not possible to doubt the existence of myself as a thinking thing. That is, even when I am being deceived about objects of perception far away, to be deceived is still to think. And even when I am dreaming, to dream is still to think. Finally, with respect to the evil genius hypothesis, the evil genius may delight in deceiving me about mathematical propositions and the like as much as he wishes, Descartes observes, but he will never deceive me to such an extent that he will cause me to think I am nothing as long as I think I am something. For to be deceived is, again, to think, so each and every time I am deceived I am nonetheless thinking. At this point Descartes has arrived at his great pillar, the foundation upon which he may begin to reconstruct his knowledge and retrieve everything he has thus far doubted. 'I think therefore I am' or '*cogito ergo sum*' becomes for him a fundamental point of departure and the principle upon which he will go on to first prove God's existence and goodness and then the existence of the world (by arguing that God exists and is good and that, therefore, would not deceive us that the world as we perceive it exists as we perceive it). The cogito, he demonstrates, is nothing other than 'a thinking thing' or 'a thing that thinks' which broadly includes for him the act of willing, imagining, understanding and feeling. Importantly, Descartes' programme of the reconstruction of our knowledge and his strategy of systematic doubt require him to investigate the *activity* of the cogito as an essentially *thinking* activity that will then give him the tools he needs to prove the existence and goodness of God, and ultimately the existence of the world itself.

iii. SARTRE'S DEBT TO DESCARTES

Now that we have sketched Descartes' stages of systematic doubt and subsequent claim that he exists as a thinking thing, we are ready to appreciate the unique influence Descartes' method and strategy had on Sartre, both directly and indirectly. We may readily find Sartre's own acknowledgement of debt to Descartes in a short essay titled 'Cartesian Freedom' and we will rely on it primarily to illustrate both Sartre's praise for and critique of Descartes.

In this short but illuminating essay, Sartre initially asserts that

> Freedom is one and indivisible, but it manifests itself according to circumstances. The following question may be asked of all philosophers who set up as its defenders: in connection with what exceptional situation have you experienced your freedom? It is one thing to test your freedom in the realm of action, of social or political activity, or of artistic creation, and another thing to test it in the act of understanding and discovering. (Sartre 1962: 180)

Descartes, of course, was testing freedom in the act of understanding and discovering the power of the mind to apprehend itself. And this is why, Sartre observes, 'we Frenchmen, who have been living by Cartesian freedom for three centuries, understand implicitly by "free will" the practice of independent *thinking* rather than the production of a creative act . . .' (Sartre 1962: 180). Free will could not be the production of a creative act because thought itself had to have, he notes, '*something* to understand, whether it be the objective relationships among essences and among structures, or the sequence of ideas, in short, a pre-established order of relationships' (Sartre 1962: 181). The great intuition of Descartes, notes Sartre, was that he 'was more fully aware than anyone else that the slightest act of thinking involves all thinking, an autonomous thinking that posits itself – in each of its acts – in full and absolute independence' (Sartre 1962: 181). As a seventeenth-century mathematician, Descartes was confronted with the view that 'the order of mathematical truths seemed to all right-thinking people the product of the divine will' and he felt compelled to save subjectivity from the clutches of the objective order of the time, with God at the top relegating all subordinate truths to their rightful place.[1] Confronted with an impotent subjectivity whose only power was to 'adhere to the true' and observe the strict order of essences, Descartes recognized more than anyone else that there could be 'no difference between thought and truth' and that 'true is the totality of the system of thoughts' (Sartre 1962: 182). It is precisely in his recognition and awareness of the impotent subjectivity of his age that Sartre so admired in Descartes, as well as his ingenious solution to a lost subjectivity in the clutches of Catholic orthodoxy: 'If anyone wants to save man, the only thing to do, since he cannot produce any idea but only contemplate it, is to provide him with a simple negative power, that of saying no to whatever is not true' (Sartre 1962: 182). Here, Sartre is alluding to Cartesian methodical doubt, as detailed above, that systematically calls all truths into question by doubting, in an effort to build a new foundation from which Descartes could then recover everything he had doubted.

Notably, Sartre credits Descartes with not only restoring human subjectivity to its rightful place, but also with affirming the responsibility of persons:

> His spontaneous reaction is to affirm the responsibility of man in the presence of the true. Truth is a human thing, since I must affirm it in order for it to exist. Before my *judgment*, which is an adherence of my will and a free commitment of my being, there exist only neutral and floating ideas which are neither true nor false. Man is thus the being through whom truth appears in the world . . . Descartes therefore begins by providing us with entire intellectual responsibility. (Sartre 1962: 182–3)

Here, Sartre's praise of Descartes should not be underestimated; he relates Descartes' innovation to another important philosophical influence, the German philosopher Martin Heidegger's claim concerning one's death: 'As Heidegger has said, nobody can die for me. But Descartes had said earlier that nobody can understand for me. In the end, we must say yes or no and decide alone, for the entire universe, on what is true' (Sartre 1962: 183). The Cartesian recognition of the importance of human affirmation and negation, even amidst a world of established essences and structures pre-ordained by the God of the seventeenth century, was enough, notes Sartre, for ensuring our metaphysical freedom as an absolute act and commitment. Moreover, the Cartesian recognition of thinking as autonomous established human freedom as total, and not merely a 'matter of degree':

> . . . it belongs equally to every man. Or rather—for freedom is not a quality among other qualities—it is evident that every man is a freedom . . . A man cannot be more of a man than other men because freedom is similarly infinite in each individual. In this sense no one has shown better than Descartes the connection between the spirit of science and the spirit of democracy, for universal suffrage cannot be founded on anything other than this universal faculty of saying yes or saying no. (Sartre 1962: 184–5)

The differences in mental and physical strengths and weaknesses that exist among persons are, Sartre notes, corporeal accidents: 'The only thing that characterizes us as human creatures is the use that we freely make of these gifts . . . the situation of a man and his powers cannot increase or limit his freedom' (Sartre 1962: 184). Here, Sartre credits Descartes, after the Stoics, with having distinguished freedom and power: 'To be free is not to be able to do what one wants but to want what one can' (Sartre 1962: 184). Sartre wholeheartedly endorses this distinction and the point can not be made more strongly that, contra his most stubborn critics, he *never* offered the absurd definition of freedom as 'absolute' in the sense that one can do whatever one wants. He observes, on the contrary, 'with a variable and limited power, man has total freedom' (Sartre 1962: 184). Sartre recognizes that while freedom maintains a positive, constructive 'efficacity', it has a negative side in that 'it probably cannot change the quality of the movement that is in the world, but it can modify the direction of this movement' (Sartre 1962: 185). He locates the origin of the 'efficacity' and constructiveness of freedom in another of Descartes' works, namely, *Discourse on Method*, because Descartes *invented* the method: 'Certain paths', says Descartes, 'have led me to considerations and maxims from which I have formed a method' (Sartre 1962: 185). Sartre then proceeds to show how Descartes' rules are at once creative and inventive acts of judgement:

> They represent, in sum, very general directives for free and creative judgment ... We thus discover in his works a splendid humanistic affirmation of creative freedom, which constructs the true, piece by piece, which at every moment anticipates and prefigures the real relationships among essences by producing hypotheses and schemata which equal for God and for man, equal for all men, absolute and infinite, forces us to assume a fearful task, our task par excellence, namely, to cause a truth to exist in the world, to act so that the world is true—and which causes us to live with generosity, a 'sentiment that each one has of his own free will and that is joined to the resolution never to be lacking in it'. (Sartre 1962: 185–6)

Despite the fact that the Cartesian will is forced to affirm or adhere to the 'irresistible' evidence of the rigorous structure that is presented to his mind so clearly and distinctly, and despite Descartes' faith in God such that his 'entire will is shot through and illuminated by an inner and supernatural light that is called grace' (Sartre 1962: 188), Sartre maintains that, for Descartes, there is really not a 'great difference between natural light and this supernatural light which is grace' (Sartre 1962: 188). It is at this juncture that Sartre discovers in Descartes the seeds of the crucial idea of nothingness that he develops in his own philosophy:

> If I am irresistibly inclined to affirm the idea, it is exactly insofar as it weighs on me with all its being and all its absolute positiveness. It is this pure and dense being, flawless and entire, which affirms itself within me by its own weight. Thus, since god is the source of all being and all positivity, this positivity, this fullness of existence which is itself a true judgment, cannot have its source in me, who am nothing, but in Him . . . It expresses, in the

vocabulary of the time, the consciousness that the scientist has always had of being a pure nothingness, a simple beholder in the face of the obstinate and eternal consistency, the infinite weight of the truth he contemplates. (Sartre 1962: 188)

Sartre affirms this Cartesian idea by devoting an entire chapter to it in *Being and Nothingness*, titled 'The Power of Negation', which we will discuss in Chapter 4. In Cartesian Freedom, Sartre notes that the power of negation Descartes confers on the will (through methodical doubt), coupled with his view that God has placed everything that is positive within me and is the author of who I am, establishes autonomy as a *refusal* rather than as creative invention:

> . . . I who am a nothingness, can say no to all these nothingnesses (e.g., to fragmentary, obscure, or uncertain ideas). I am able not to decide to act or affirm. Since the order of truths exists outside of me, that which will define me as an autonomy is not creative invention but refusal. It is by refusing to the point of being unable to refuse any more that we are free. Thus, methodical doubt becomes the very model of the free act. (Sartre 1962: 189–90)

For Sartre, the Cartesian 'order of truths that exist outside of me' become relics of the seventeenth-century mindset that could only be partially challenged by Descartes. It would be up to Sartre to exercise his own negating power by claiming that the free act, in its very refusal, is creative and inventive; for Descartes such a move would have been too radical, given the power of the Church and, indeed, Descartes' own constraints as a man of faith. As an atheist, Sartre would extend this Cartesian insight by claiming that our freedom is not merely refusal or negation, but also creative and inventive since, in the absence of any putative God or eternal order of truths, 'there must be someone to invent truths' and that 'someone' must be us.

And indeed, in the closing pages of 'Cartesian Freedom', Sartre credits Descartes with having discovered not merely a negative freedom by way of systematic doubt, but also, it turns out, a creative freedom: 'But since Descartes warns us that God's freedom is no more entire than that of man and that one is in the image of the other, we have a new means of investigation . . .' (Sartre 1962: 193). Constrained by absolutely nothing and free from all imposition,

'The God of Descartes is the freest of gods that have been forged by human thought' (Sartre 1962: 194). Descartes' recognition 'that the concept of freedom involved necessarily an absolute autonomy, that a free act was an absolutely new production, the germ of which could not be contained in an earlier state of the world and that consequently freedom and creation were one and the same' allowed him to posit freedom 'as the foundation of the true' (Sartre 1962: 195) and to see that the 'root of all Reason is to be sought in the depths of the free act' (Sartre 1962: 195). Conceiving divine freedom as at once an act of intellection and an invention of the Good, Descartes, the 'dogmatic rationalist', observes Sartre, placed in God the power of willing and intuition as one and the same such that 'divine consciousness is both constitutive and contemplative' (Sartre 1962: 195). The Cartesian move that is crucial, then, is that 'the divine prerogative is, in the last analysis, an absolute freedom which invents Reason and Good . . .' (Sartre 1962: 195), and yet, 'there is nothing more in this freedom than in human freedom, and he is aware, in describing his God's free will, that he has merely developed the implicit content of the idea of freedom' (Sartre 1962: 196). Here, Sartre latches on to what he regards as the most significant and paradoxical contribution Descartes has made:

> If we examine the matter closely, we shall see that this is why human freedom is not limited by an order of freedoms and values which might offer themselves to our assent as eternal things, as necessary structures of being. It is the divine will that has laid down these values and truths and that supports them. Our freedom is limited only by divine freedom. The world is only the creation of a freedom that preserves it for an indefinite time. Truth is nothing if it is not willed by this infinite and divine power and if it is not taken up, assumed and confirmed by human freedom. The free man is alone in the face of an absolutely free God. Freedom is the foundation of being, its secret dimension. Freedom, in this rigorous system, is the inner meaning and the true face of necessity. (Sartre 1962: 196)

Thus Sartre discovers in Descartes the origins of the philosophical affirmation of human freedom and responsibility. Notwithstanding the dictatorial age in which Descartes lived, Sartre admires him for returning, following his description of divine freedom, to his own freedom, which he says is 'known without proof and merely by our experience of it' (Sartre 1962: 196). It matters little, Sartre notes, that Descartes 'was forced by the age in which he lived, as well as his point of departure, to reduce the human free will to a merely negative power to deny itself until it finally yields and abandons itself to the divine solicitude' (Sartre 1962: 196). It matters little that Descartes 'hypostasized in God the original and *constituent* freedom whose infinite existence he recognized by means of the *cogito* itself' (Sartre 1962: 196). None of this matters, Sartre says, because

The fact remains that a formidable power of divine and human affirmation runs through and supports his universe. It took two centuries of crisis—a crisis of Faith and a crisis of Science—for man to regain the creative freedom that Descartes placed in God, and for anyone to suspect the following truth, which is an essential basis of humanism: man is the being as a result of whose appearance a world exists. But we shall not reproach Descartes with having given to God that which reverts to us in our own right. Rather, we shall admire him for having, in a dictatorial age, laid the groundwork of democracy, for having followed to the very end the demands of the idea of autonomy and for having understood long before Heidegger of VomWesem des Grundes, that the sole foundation of being is freedom. (Sartre 1962: 196–7)

Here, we see Sartre's deep admiration for and indebtedness to Descartes insofar as Descartes has shown, before anyone else, the fundamental importance of human autonomy in its capacity to call the world into question and, in so doing, to creatively assume itself and its place in the world. Importantly, Sartre will extend this Cartesian insight in his own philosophy by claiming that the power of negation or, of saying 'no' or calling the world into question, are uniquely human abilities that distinguish human reality from objects and that fill our world with possibility. The ability to say no, to question, to doubt, to judge, and to experience absence are distinctly human abilities and evidence, Sartre says, of our freedom. This immediately raises the question, what kind of beings are we such that we can freely create one possible reality rather than another? *Being and Nothingness*, Sartre's most important and influential work, is principally devoted to investigating this question.

CHAPTER 4

THE HUMAN CONDITION

Therefore there is an original upsurge not of goals but of questions. The answers are not given. There is no answer. The answers are not to be found, but to be invented and chosen.

(Sartre 1992: 449)

i. OUR FREEDOM

Sartre's most important philosophical work, *Being and Nothingness: An Essay in Phenomenological Ontology* (hereafter *BN*), published in 1943, is a densely packed corpus of work that is 700 pages in length and filled both with complex, abstruse philosophical terminology and vivid, sometimes humorous examples to illustrate the ideas Sartre wishes to explain. In *BN*, Sartre synthesizes the phenomenology of Husserl (the accurate description of the objects of our conscious activity and the study of the conscious acts that reveal these objects of experience to us) and the ontology of Husserl's pupil, Heidegger (the study of the different kinds of being there are and what their structures are). In Sartre's view both philosophers made fundamental contributions, but by themselves, their contributions were incomplete. Husserl, Sartre charged, risked placing all philosophical emphasis on our conscious acts at the expense of treatment of the world of which we are conscious. In a word, Husserl's approach too closely approximated idealism, the view that the ideas in our mind represent or reflect the world and that the world is merely a representation of those ideas, which are most real (not the world). And Heidegger's study of ontology in his monumental *Being and Time* (1927), too strenuously emphasized the other side of the equation, namely, Being, thereby threatening to eclipse conscious awareness itself. Sartre's genius is that he recognized the need for both kinds of investigation, and in *BN* he attempts just such a synthesis of Husserl's and Heidegger's teachings.

Most broadly, Sartre argues in *BN* that the freedom we enjoy as agents consists in a creative and autonomous agency, not, as some critics have charged, a reckless capriciousness. Sartre convincingly argues that the freedom we have as persons is not the freedom to do anything we wish, such as fly to the moon on a whim, but rather the freedom to make and remake ourselves in a world that offers resistance and, very often, overwhelming obstacles. Sartre wishes to emphasize that we are free in a morally important sense to choose who we will become and what sort of world shall become the world.

Under the influence of Descartes, Sartre emphasizes that what is most distinctive about persons is that they are autonomous, which is to say they are uniquely capable of withdrawing from any situation with which they are presented and may always question it, doubt it, reject it, and, most importantly, change it. In Sartre's view, moreover, although we tend to take comfortable refuge in the cultural and social roles, expectations, and values we believe are imposed on us, we are, in the last analysis, always free to reject any or all of these. Thus while we may believe that we must conform to outside forces in truth, he insists, in conforming to them we choose them. Hence, what we become is always and in the first instance what we choose to become, not what is imposed upon us from outside.

We can readily appreciate the influence of both Socrates and Descartes on Sartre's perspective; through choice, reasoning, questioning, doubting and reflection, he believed that persons could determine their own moral point of view concerning what constitutes the good life. And through active self-criticism and self-questioning our beliefs, desires, habits and convictions, he thought that persons could achieve a level of personal and interpersonal wellbeing. The Socratic dictum, 'The unexamined life is not worth living' and the Cartesian maxim to 'question authority' through doubting and questioning are readily apparent here. Socrates, Descartes and Sartre were equally committed, although for different reasons, to the freedom of mind that distinguishes persons from everything else in the universe. All three philosophers were each in their own way champions of human freedom; the very possibility of examining one's life in the way Socrates urged his fellow Athenians to do, and of thinking for oneself and questioning authority as Descartes' *Meditations* does, presupposes, Sartre would surely insist, that we are free. On his view, we are never in a position of complete helplessness because there is a chasm or gap between our consciousness and the world of which we are conscious; we can always ask, even in the most difficult, seemingly impossible of situations, 'What can I do?' or 'What must I do?' We are thus never inextricably attached to the world or to the situation in which we find ourselves because our conscious activity that characterizes us as persons, as human reality, ensures that we stand back from the world or any situation with which we are confronted. Indeed, Sartre wanted no less from his philosophy than that it challenge us to change the world and he emphasized again and again, and in multiple ways, that it is only *we* who can change the world for better or worse, that it is only *we* who can reject those who say 'No, we can't' or shouldn't try, support those who say 'Yes, we can' and should try, and, even at great risk to ourselves, join those who say 'Yes, we must and we will.' There is, for Sartre, always a cause greater than ourselves, and that cause is the cause of creating, individually and collectively, a flourishing humanity in a world of formidable obstacles and uncertainty.

Importantly for Sartre, although we are free to choose *who* we are, we are not free to choose *what* we are. It is in this sense that our freedom involves a certain paradox because we are not free not to be free; the underside of our freedom is its necessity in a contingent world of possibility. Of equal importance, Sartre recognizes that our freedom is obviously constrained and conditioned by given determinants, such as biological, psychological, physical and historical conditions, what he calls, following Heidegger, 'facticity' (which is why I cannot fly to the moon right now on a whim or decide suddenly to become a world class chess player). Sartre of course recognizes that insofar as we are embodied and situated in the natural world, we are subject to natural laws, to the general causal determinism of the natural world. Insofar as we are situated in this time and space, then, with certain motivations, emotions, desires and values, Sartre grants that we are indeed determined in *that* sense. Importantly, Sartre does not, in point of fact, claim that human consciousness is totally separated from nature because consciousness is always embodied; in this respect his views are opposed in a rather significant way to those of Plato, Descartes and Kant, who claim that there is a dimension of human consciousness that exists apart from nature and is therefore immune from natural causal laws. As we will see, and here Sartre is in agreement with Kant, the whole issue of human freedom is about our *subjectivity*, not about the lack of causal determination; Sartre does not claim that persons, as embodied subjects, are immune from the laws of nature. So in a sense Sartre escapes the age-old freewill-determinism debate by changing the subject; he is not interested in participating in that debate. What he *is* interested in is asking how persons see themselves in a particular situation in the world and in relation to other people. Do they view themselves as agents of change or as mere pawns of the universe? Do they passively acquiesce to oppression and injustice, or do they fight against these? These are the questions that interested him and they are also the questions that interested Socrates.

And yet, because Sartre argues that consciousness is *nothing* (about which we shall have more to say shortly), we are never *wholly* determined or exhaustively caused in the way that natural objects are; the laws of physics can never get a hold of us as they get a hold of falling bodies, precisely because our conscious activity drives a gap between us and the laws that govern the rest of the universe. Again, we are always able to take a point of view on our situation, to question it, doubt it, affirm it, and so on; it never announces itself once and for all. We are always free, moreover, to make more out of what has *already* been made of us. Since it is always up to us to freely *make* of our situation what we will, nothing is ever wholly determined for us, but rather everything presents itself to us as an opportunity to embrace, to dismiss as irrelevant, to go beyond, to ignore, or to forget.

For Sartre, then, what I am (now) as expressed (now) in this chosen action is my (present) 'personal identity', and that is *formed* by me. It is in this sense that he claims that we are not determined by our characters, our past, our biology or by the impersonal forces of history. And as much as we might want to insist that we are so determined, Sartre reminds us of our uniquely human ability to always question or challenge the meaning that our 'character', our past, our biology or the impersonal forces of history might have for us. In this regard *nothing*, on Sartre's account, can ever be self-announcing, independent of the signification I choose to confer on it.[1] We are unique, then, precisely because we are capable of determining ourselves by our own choice, purposes and reasons. Sartre thus maintains that we contribute, through our own intentions, actions and choices to who we are as agents in the world; in a morally significant sense, then, we are the authors of our own lives and the captains of our own ships.

Another way to appreciate Sartre's meaning is to say that if there is any determinism it could only be the sense in which we determine ourselves. Hence our beliefs, desires, convictions, emotions, and motivational dispositions are not given to us as properties or as unchangeable natural characteristics – like our skin colour or height, all of which, again, Sartre calls 'facticity', – because they describe certain 'facts' about us. These qualities do not belong to us like oxygen belongs to water. Sartre claims, rather, that we have a *relation* to our beliefs, desires and emotions; we are capable of taking a point of view with respect to them and to reflect explicitly upon them and, hence, to deny or affirm them. So just in the same way whatever situation we are in can never exhaustively determine what we will do or not do because it is we who must interpret the meaning the situation has for us; our qualities or attributes are not, in Sartre's view, self-announcing because it is always up to us to determine what meaning they have for us. Persons, then, differ from objects in that they are not merely composed of certain qualities that make them what they are; indeed, Sartre notes that while the principle of identity in logic applies to objects or to non-human reality ('A is A in virtue of being itself and *not* anything else') it does not apply to human reality because persons can always be *other* than what they are at any given moment. A whicker chair just *is* a whicker chair; a plank of wood just *is* a plank of wood and a crayon just *is* a crayon. But persons are always *more* than what they appear to be because, in addition to having certain qualities and 'given' characteristics (facticity), they are also constituted by their possibilities and projects and, moreover, those possibilities and projects colour and modify whatever is given to us antecedently. Sartre attempted to capture this idea in his famous *Existentialism is a humanism* speech in Paris with the slogan, 'Existence precedes essence', suggesting that we are born and exist first in the world and then later define ourselves or create our essence; our essence is not given antecedently, rather, it is perpetually made and re-made by us throughout our lives. Here what is essential to grasp is that the most important questions in our lives are worked out by existing, not by playing out a script or following a rulebook. Sartre claims, then, that persons are free precisely in the sense that they are not exhaustively or essentially characterized by certain 'givens', but they are also constituted by their possibilities, by what they are aiming at, and they may thus ask morally relevant questions concerning who they are, what they want to become, and what they *should* become, both individually and collectively. And to ask *these* kinds of questions is to exercise a capacity that is peculiar to human beings, and to suggest that persons may be responsible for their lives (and, importantly, the lives of others) in a unique sort of way.

While we have seen that Sartre admires Descartes' discovery that human consciousness is uniquely capable of doubting what is presented to it, he takes this Cartesian insight a step further in extending its importance to questions of meaning and value. That is, while Descartes was largely preoccupied in his *Meditations* with engaging in systematic doubt to discover a fundamental, indubitable bedrock upon which he could reconstruct all further knowledge, Sartre is concerned in *BN* to ask how our uniquely human ability to question, doubt, affirm and deny creates a world that is meaningful and has value. How does our capacity to question, doubt, deny and affirm carve meaning into the world and thereby alter its landscape? Sartre fastens on to the critical Cartesian insight that consciousness is active in its ability to doubt ('Contrary to what was claimed by the Bush Administration, did the terrorism on US soil in point of fact have any relation to Iraq?'), and extends it to the reflexive capacity of consciousness to ask critical questions about our humanity ('What does it *mean* to be a citizen in the twenty-first century?'), to step back and reflect ('In what ways may I reduce my carbon footprint and help ameliorate global warming and further environmental degradation?') or, to use Sartre's language, to effect a 'rupture' with what we are given in a world that resists us (human rights are never *given* to a people by government; they have to be won, and very often won through long, painful struggle and agitation). What are we going to do with our lives? What kind of world do we want to create? What values are most important? What is the meaning of our humanity? Why are these questions important to us? In *BN*, Sartre delineates two specific regions of Being that elucidate the importance of our relation to the world in which we live and serve as a crucial point of departure in answering these questions. We will consider this ontological division next.

ii. TWO REGIONS OF BEING

It is important to note that Sartre subtitles *BN* 'An Essay in Phenomenological Ontology'. What does this mean? Recall that the study of *ontology* involves the elucidation or description of the kinds of being that there are in the world. In offering an ontological investigation, then, Sartre is interested in exploring the different modes of existence that a particular kind of being may have, as well as its relationship to other kinds of being. Sartre offers an ontological description of at least two kinds of being that may be said to exist, being in-itself or non-conscious being and being for-itself, or conscious being. In offering a *phenomenological* study, Sartre is attempting to describe the central structures of *lived experience* (le vécu); in this sense the entire book is a structural analysis of the phenomenon of human experiencing, a phenomenon which is always already an implicit 'self-experiencing', since for Sartre, as we will see, our conscious awareness of ourselves as free is always present, at least implicitly. In an important sense, Sartre is seeking to uncover the nature of lived experience. The term 'uncover' suggests that he thinks our experience has been systematically concealed, especially by other philosophers in the tradition who have eclipsed our lived experience in their attempts to understand the nature of reality, knowledge and God. Here, Sartre again follows Heidegger in claiming that much of our western philosophical thinking has been done solely with regard to our already instituted reflective standpoint. For example, both Plato and Aristotle are already well within a certain reflective standpoint in their respective accounts of reality and, in this respect, they have, as it were, put the cart before the horse since they have ignored the lived human experience that necessarily precedes philosophical reflection. Heidegger and Sartre object that this reflective focus has not only eclipsed our lived experience as such, but has also altered or 'veiled' the reality of our lived experience. As a result, philosophy has been for the most part deeply misguided because it has put reflective theory before experience and, hence, too often, the reflective theory has been shown to be contradictory to or even against experience.

In large part, then, *BN* is an attempt to recover the realities of lived experience, and to reveal the meaning of human existence as lived experience. For both Heidegger and Sartre, the term 'recover' suggests that something has been lost. This is indeed

Sartre's point: our lived experience has been lost in the folds of philosophical reflection. But, importantly, this is not to deny that *BN* expresses a reflective standpoint's discoveries; as a study in phenomenological ontology, *BN* elucidates the *conditions under which human experience*, and especially for Sartre, the conditions under which human *moral* experience, is possible. What are the possibilities of, especially, the moral dimension of human experience?

Returning now to the fundamental ontological distinction Sartre makes in *BN* between being in-itself and being for-itself, we should note that Sartre is especially concerned to show how persons are fundamentally distinct from objects and to understand what this distinction means with respect to how we experience ourselves in the world. Among the ways we experience ourselves in the world are through certain 'existential emotions' such as anguish, forlornness, despair, a feeling of abandonment and even joy. Sartre thus forges this distinction to establish, on the one hand, non-experiencing (non-conscious) material objects, which he calls 'in-itself being', and experiencing (conscious) beings which he calls 'for-itself being'.

Sartre's description of material objects as complete, self-sufficient, full, brute and inert suggests that they simply are *there*, obtrusively imposing themselves in the world; 'Being is what it is', Sartre tells us in *BN* (Sartre 1956: 29). This is the region of being that is famously disclosed to the protagonist Roquentin, in Sartre's most well-known philosophical novel, *Nausea* (1938). Roquentin feels himself 'de trop' or superfluous in the midst of Being; his nausea and boredom reveal to him the contingency of everything that exists around him, including himself:

And I—soft, weak, obscene, digesting, juggling with dismal thoughts—I, too, was *In the way*. Fortunately, I didn't feel it, although I realized it. But I was uncomfortable because I was afraid—(even now I am afraid—afraid that it might catch me behind my head and lift me up like a wave). I dreamed vaguely of killing myself to wipe out at least one of these superfluous lives. But even my death would have been *In the way*. In the way, my corpse, my blood on these stones, between these plants, at the back of this smiling garden. And the decomposed flesh would have been *In the way* in the earth which would receive my bones, at last, cleaned, stripped, peeled, proper and clean as teeth, it would have been *In the way*: I was *In the way* for eternity. (Sartre 1964: 128–9)

Here, Sartre lucidly describes the sheer, brute experience of existence; for Roquentin everything, including his bodily self is 'in the way' because it has no reason to exist in itself, but must await the imprint of conscious activity to become meaningful. Absent the imprint of conscious activity on objects, objects may only enjoy a gratuitous existence. Material objects, then, need not worry about sustaining themselves or about becoming; they simply are what they are. Like the chestnut tree that Sartre describes in *Nausea*, material objects 'overflow' with a superfluity of being:

> So I was in the park just now. The roots of the chestnut tree were sunk in the ground just under my bench. I couldn't remember if it was a root anymore. The words had vanished and with them the significance of things, their methods of use, and the feeble points of reference which men have traced on their surface. I was sitting, stooping forward, head bowed alone in front of this black, knotty mass, entirely beastly, which frightened me . . . this root, with its color, shape, its congealed movement, was . . . below all explanation. Each of its qualities escaped it a little, flowed out of it, half solidified, almost became a thing: each one was *In the way* in the root and the whole stump now gave me the impression of unwinding itself a little, denying its existence to lose itself in a frenzied excess. (Sartre 1964: 128–9)

Here, we can appreciate the descriptive force of Sartre's characterization of the region of being that is not conscious, or 'in-itself being' as brute and inert as just there, in the way.

Sartre demarcates this region of being in order to distinguish it from another kind of being, namely human being, or 'for itself being'. This is the kind of being we are, of course, the kind of being who has experiences, and who is, moreover, implicitly aware of having those experiences. Sartre maintains that persons, as 'conscious activity', have distinctive features exactly opposed to those of material objects. We have seen that the principle of identity (that a table is a table and not anything else) holds for material objects, but not for persons. For Sartre this is absolutely crucial. As experiencing beings persons are never complete, never self-sufficient, and never inert and brute. Persons are the kind of beings who can take a point of view on the world, distance themselves from the world, question and negate the world, and reject or affirm a state of affairs in the world. Persons are always 'on the move'; they are always self-transcending in that they may always go beyond the present and hurl themselves into a future of unlimited possibilities (it is no wonder that Sartre claims that our freedom is also experienced in joy!). To say that persons are self-transcending is to say that they are able to formulate projects and ambitions, imagine alternative possibilities, plan ahead and create themselves in particular kinds of ways. Indeed, prior to *BN* Sartre had already published two works on imagination, both of which investigate the power of the imagination to create and thereby conceive of a different kind of world. Sartre distinguishes persons, then, as projects and possibilities, not as things; they create themselves by actively changing their situation in the world, and the power of their imagination plays a key role in what kind of world might be possible. Moreover, unlike material objects which, we have seen, have a kind of 'full-ness' and 'thereness' about them, persons are 'empty' and always ahead of themselves as they project themselves into a future that is in the making. Unlike material objects, persons experience the world, and this experience involves continually creating themselves so that they may become something. While it is the very nature of material objects that the principle of identity holds, persons, para-doxically, must perpetually engage in a project of becoming in order to retain identity.

Life for us, according to Sartre, is the sum total of choices we have made and will continue to make until we die. Life is a project, a task, an undertaking, and an effort. Goals may be met, but to keep them in view, we must constantly sustain and undertake them as *projects*. I may have the goal and dream to run the Boston mara-thon, but this goal will remain a mirage unless I hold it in view by training for it; it will remain alive as a goal as long as I attend to it through my daily choices as it awaits my effort to achieve it. Similarly, persons may project goals in order to express certain ideals, such as the ideal of telling the truth or the ideal of giving back more than one receives, but Sartre reminds us that the ideals themselves require our continual commitment in order for them to be sustained as ideals. In this sense persons can never be complete or self-sustained; they can never simply be what they seek to be.

They must, through their own efforts, always make and re-make themselves in a world that will guarantee them nothing.[2]

Following Heidegger, Sartre holds that, as experiencing beings, we reveal or disclose non-conscious being (in-itself being), are dependent on being, and (importantly) do not create being. This last point is especially crucial in light of some critics' objections that Sartre's commitment to freedom is so radical that it allows us to create anything we want, as though our freedom were not tethered to the world and to others in crucial ways. Rather than creating anything we want Sartre advances the far more plausible claim that our relation to being is such that we can modify it: 'It is not given to "human reality" to annihilate even provisionally the mass of being which it posits before itself. Man's *relation* with being is that (we) can modify it' (Sartre 1956: 59–60). This idea is powerfully illustrated in *Nausea*, where Roquentin, upon encountering the chestnut tree root, actually experiences nausea. Why? Because he realizes that it is he who must reveal the chestnut tree as it is before him, as well as being in general. 'Nausea' is just the human person's apprehension of *having to reveal being* . . . as existing *in order to* reveal being. Importantly, this *having to reveal being* is one of the ways Sartre thinks we apprehend ourselves as freedom. Outside of our own revelation there is nothing but the brute inertness of the being of material objects that is revealed to us as both the condition and necessity of revelation: being must be there in order for us to be able to reveal it. Since we apprehend ourselves as freedom without a goal or without a *given* that we are *for* (because, as freedom, we are always in the making), our revelation is accompanied by a feeling of anguish. We realize in anguish, Sartre claims, that *we* are the ones who have to reveal being and make ourselves in the midst of being.

Now that we have established Sartre's ontological demarcation between two regions of being, namely, being as conscious activity (persons) and being as non-conscious existence (material objects and the natural world), and indicated that conscious activity reveals non-conscious existence, we need to ask how, exactly, persons reveal being. The first thing to notice is that for Sartre to reveal being is to act. One of Sartre's most important insights is that we are never passive in our existence, although, he notes, in bad faith we tend to think of ourselves as passive (we will discuss the phenomenon of bad faith in a subsequent section). Persons, we have seen, are distinguished from things precisely by the fact that they engage in an activity that is peculiar to them, namely, the activity of revealing and, moreover, Sartre insists that we are implicitly aware of this activity of revealing in the sense that we are always implicitly reflexive, or implicitly aware of ourselves as revealing the world as it stands before us; this is one of the ways in which we apprehend ourselves as free.

iii. THE PROCESS OF NEGATION: DISCLOSING AND REVEALING THE WORLD AND THE SELF

In Chapter 3, we noted the ways in which Sartre was greatly influenced by Descartes. In particular we saw that Sartre praised Descartes for having discovered the importance of doubting and questioning in our conscious activity; our ability to withdraw from the world we are in and to question it, negate it, doubt it, affirm it or deny it are all uniquely human abilities. Sartre seizes upon this Cartesian insight and offers a phenomenological analysis of it in *BN* in a chapter titled 'The Process of Negation'. Indeed, one of Sartre's most important contributions to philosophy is his analysis of conscious activity as negation as the process by which we reveal the world of objects that stand over against us. Because our conscious activity is a dynamic process by which we reveal or disclose the world and its objects, Sartre claims that there is nothing in our conscious activity that we can point to or fix upon; consciousness is, quite simply, nothing (hence the title of his book, '*Being and Nothingness*'). Our conscious activity is, importantly, dependent on being, but is not itself being (since it is a 'no-thing' that relates to the being – the world – upon which it depends). Here, we can see clearly how 'being' for Sartre must be the *condition* of all revelation: in order for my revelation of the world to be possible, there must *be something* to reveal and, following Heidegger, Sartre calls this something 'being'.

Notably Simone de Beauvoir not only influenced Sartre's thinking on numerous philosophical issues and problems, but extended and developed some of his seminal ideas, often articulating them more clearly than Sartre. With respect the process of negation, for example, de Beauvoir captures the peculiar moral significance of our ability to 'make ourselves a lack so there might be being':

Sartre tells us that man makes himself a lack of being in order that there might be being. The term in order that clearly indicates an intentionality. It is not in vain that main nullifies being. Thanks to him, being is disclosed and he desires this disclosure. There is an original type of attachment to being which is not the relationship of 'wanting to be' but rather 'wanting to disclose being.' Now, here there is not failure, but rather success. This end, which man proposes to himself by making himself a lack of being, is in effect, realized by him. (de Beauvoir 1991: 12)

As de Beauvoir notes, to say that persons 'make themselves a lack of being in order that there might be being' is another way of saying that persons are able to *disclose* the world by calling it into question. Here again, the influence of Descartes is readily apparent. As a process that negates or withdraws from the world, our conscious activity forges a gap or chasm between what we find and what might be created in the world. Unlike material objects, persons are able to stand back or withdraw from the world by what Sartre calls a 'nihilating movement'. This nihilating movement allows the world to be revealed in a particular way, and creates the possibility for it to be changed.

Our 'sense of self', in Sartre's view, is not to be understood as a 'pure positivity' in the sense that Plato and Kant understood it, for example, as positively identified as wholly rational, or as Hume understood it as positively identified as sensible. Our sense of self is rather to be understood as a *negativity* because we are at a distance from ourselves since our conscious awareness drives a gap between us and the world. Hence Sartre's slogan 'that human reality, in its most immediate being . . . must be what it is not and not be what it is' (Sartre 1956: 112) conveys that my sense of self is precisely my ability to nihilate the world by questioning and doubting it (I *am* just this nihilating activity in relation to the world) and I am not whatever I claim to be in any definitive sense since I can always negate it and choose to be something else). And this activity is ongoing because it is not what we *are*, but what we *do* that ultimately defines us. Hence de Beauvoir remarks paradoxically, that we can only coincide with ourselves 'by agreeing never to rejoin' ourselves (de Beauvoir 1991: 33). Recall again that the principle of identity fails to hold for persons because they are always self-distancing; it is in this sense that they are free. Through this self-distancing, through this rupture of the self in relation to the world, both the world and the self will be disclosed, created and revealed. Through this self-distancing both the world and the self can change – for better or worse.

The negative condition that distinguishes persons not only helps us to see the way in which persons can question and so disclose the world, but it also provides for Sartre a basis for the possibility of *not* being what one is. So, for example, one is not a student, an artist or a waiter in the sense that a glass is a glass; again, where persons are concerned, the principle of identity fails to hold. I may be a physician rather than an engineer or astronomer, but only in the mode of not being one. In principle, and this is again the sense in which we are free, I may decide at any time that I no longer want to be physician. The very condition of not being a physician is created by the fact that I am (now) one and not anything else. There is, moreover, in Sartre's view the ever-present possibility of changing a role, even while one is engaged in it; a physician may decide, quite suddenly, that she must step away from her profession on the spot, and leave her office. The fact that we can make ourselves a lack or, as Sartre says, that for human reality 'nothingness lies coiled in the heart of Being', shows us that the self we are is constantly seeking to become the self we wish to create and that our process of making ourselves is never in vain precisely because, as a manifestation of freedom, it is creative and inventive.

Importantly for Sartre, conscious activity's introduction of negation into the world not only separates conscious activity from the world of which it is a part, but also depends on that world in order to negate. The point is that we cannot just create negations willy-nilly or *ex nihilio*; real negations are created against a foundation in one's real life; individuals confront circumstances that limit their choices and condition their possibilities in felt ways. So, for example, I cannot right this minute realistically become a famous opera singer, although I can create other possibilities. There is, Sartre insists, a real 'coefficient of adversity' (an expression he borrowed from the philosopher Gaston Bachelard), or *resistance* that I meet with in the world, and that I will not be able to surpass, an assertion that reinforces Sartre's commitment to direct realism, the view that the world of things exists independently of our awareness of them. And, in fact, the world is shot through with resistance, as anyone who has seen the sign, 'Keep off the grass' is familiar with.

Applying for a slot in a very competitive university or professional organization and then being rejected is a familiar experience almost everyone has had. The world and its inhabitants say 'no' to us, just as we say 'no' to them. Moreover, the world or, better, nature itself presents itself as an obstacle to us that may or may not be overcome. While we cannot simply will away an earthquake or hurricane, we nonetheless, in Sartre's view, introduce negation into the world when we proclaim 'The earthquake destroyed the school-house.' Thus when Sartre makes the hyperbolic statement that 'It is a man who destroys his cities through the agency of earthquakes . . . and who destroys his ships through the agency of cyclones' (Sartre, *Being Nothingness*, 8–9), he is making a conceptual rather than a causal claim. He is saying that these real forces of nature cannot be called 'destruction' except through reference to a witness who can 'nihilate' the city or ship by recalling how it used to be before the earthquake or cyclone struck. Only persons, who both are able to make themselves a lack (the very meaning of our freedom that allows us to become other than what we are) and to see absence in the world, can assert that the city or ship is no longer. In itself, the earthquake is only capable of redistributing matter, such as build-ings and bridges; without a person's nihilating judgement, an earthquake or cyclone is not 'destructive'. Importantly, and this is also what makes Sartre a realist as opposed to an idealist, the redistribution of matter had to have also occurred in order for 'destruction' to be possible. The nihilating activity of which per-sons, and only persons are capable, is thus a necessary, but not a sufficient condition for destruction. The process of negation is of course a very Cartesian idea; the confrontation between our free conscious awareness – which includes our imagination, our emo-tions, our ability to judge and question – and the obstinate resist-ance of the world is the very starting point in Sartre's philosophy.

Perhaps the most important point to remember with regard to viewing persons as making themselves a lack or a 'no-thing' in their ability to carve meaning in the world through their nihilating activ-ity is that the possibility of radically changing one's life always exists. Even something we may think of as wholly determined, such as our sexuality is, in Sartre's view, *constituted* by us. Biological constitution is not sufficient in his view to constitute the meaning of our sexuality because we always freely adopt an attitude with respect to it. Transgendered persons, for example, have contested their sexual identity at birth and changed it. Gay men and lesbians have contested the social meaning of their genders and the entire construction of the traditional family, subsequently creating loving and fulfilling families of their own in same-sex partnerships. Sartre's thinking is decidedly strong here, and those who have insisted that sexual orientation is not a choice have very often misunderstood, simplified or distorted his views. In Sartre's view, sexual orientation is a choice that each individual makes for herself; biological conditions, or even the future discovery of the so-called 'gay-gene' would not, on his view, be sufficient to determine one's sexual orientation. It would not be sufficient for the simple reason that one's sense of self is not exhaustively constituted by one's genetic or biological blueprint. In Sartre's view, sexuality is also a social, cultural and political construct and, as such, it will always have a *dynamic* meaning that is mediated by persons. Here, our chosen relationship to our body is such that our body is *lived* in such a way that it becomes for us an instrument in a world of possibilities. Hence, on Sartre's account we 'exist our body' or the body 'exists itself' in a way that will determine our relationship to the world. My body, Sartre says, is 'lived and not known', underscoring the importance that the body has for him as the instrument of our projects. Notably, the body as lived and not known precludes for Sartre the very possibility Cartesian doubting that I have a body. As a phenomenologist, Sartre insists that I am intimately aware my body and I live or 'exist' it in a completely unified fashion. Here, accusations, most notably by feminist philosophers and commentators, that Sartre endorses Cartesian mind–body dualism are without foundation.

Our ability to nihilate, then, allows us to structure the meaning of our selfhood, but not once and for all; the choice to re-make the self I have made always exists on the horizon: the principle of identity fails to hold. Just as I have constituted, for example, the meaning of my sexuality in the past, I must maintain it or alter in the future if I so choose. I must hold its meaning in existence, recognizing that it could always be other than it is, although I may think that the possibility for change is remote and unlikely.

On Sartre's view, to say that persons make themselves a lack, or that they are able to engage in a nihilating activity which precludes the principle of identity from holding, is to say that persons are free. And the manifestation of freedom as negation, he says, is also evident in our attempts to hide from ourselves in bad faith our own freedom, or to limit and deny the freedom of others. So not only are we able to reveal the world and ourselves but, importantly for morality, we are also able to reveal others: '. . . consciousness is not restricted to *envisioning negations*. It constitutes itself in its own flesh as the nihilation of a possibility which another human reality projects as its possibility . . . it is as a Not that the slave first apprehends the master, or that the prisoner who is trying to escape sees the guard who is watching him' (Sartre 1956: 47) Following Hegel Sartre recognizes that our freedom is circumscribed and limited by the way others see us: it is through the eyes of the master that the slave apprehends himself as lacking humanity and it is this image he sees through the eyes of his master that he makes his own.

iv. THE INFLUENCE OF HUSSERL: INTENTIONALITY AND SELF-AWARENESS

In the short monograph *The Transcendence of the Ego* (hereafter '*TE*'), written in 1934 while he was studying phenomenology in Berlin, Sartre both embraces and distances himself from the teachings of Husserl, the founder of the phenomenological movement. Sartre fully endorses Husserl's doctrine of intentionality, the view that our conscious activity *intends* objects that stand over against us: when we are aware, we are always aware of *something*. When we imagine, for example, there is an object of our imagining (a dream vacation in Greece, for example); when we are afraid, there is an object of our fear (a car that suddenly turns in front of us); when we are joyful, there is an object of our joy (passing a competitive examination). The central teaching here is that our conscious activity always takes an object; we experience our conscious awareness as intending or aiming at something *outside* of us. In his 1939 article, 'Intentionality: A Fundamental Idea of Husserl's Phenomenology', Sartre powerfully advances the view that our intention of objects outside of us firmly establishes the existence of a world that *is* outside of us. Importantly, Sartre counters other philosophical views in the tradition that held that the mind was a kind of container and the ideas in our mind represented the world and its objects, never coming into contact with the world itself. On this view the mind assimilates objects, and sucks them up into its own conceptual architecture. Sartre dramatically depicts this view by comparing the mind to a spider that 'trap(s) things in its web, covers them with a white spit and slowly swallows them, reducing them to its own substance' ('Intentionality: A Fundamental Idea of Husserl's Phenomenology,' trans. Joseph P. Fell, Journal of the British Society for Phenomenology 1, no. 2 (May 1970) [1939]: 4). Recall that phenomenology asks us to describe both the objects of our experience as they appear to us in experience and the conscious activity through which those objects are revealed to us, we may readily appreciate the force of this comparison. Sartre maintains that, contrary to other philosophical views, we come into contact with objects directly, not indirectly, because our conscious activity is immediately intentional. In his view, our conscious activity is a 'no-thing' since it is neither a container for ideas, nor a thing itself; it is, rather,

> clear as a strong wind. There is nothing in it but a movement of fleeing itself, a sliding beyond itself. If, impossible though it be, you could enter "into" consciousness you would be seized by a whirlwind and thown back outside, in the thick of the dust, near the tree, for consciousness has no 'inside.' It is just this being beyond itself, this absolute flight, this refusal to be a substance which makes it a consciousness. (INT, 4–5)

Our conscious activity, then, 'shoots' forth and 'bursts' towards whatever it intends, 'tearing' itself from the world of which it is a part. It actively aims at something outside of itself and thereby comes into direct contact with the world: 'You see this tree, to be sure. But you see it just where it is: at the side of the road, in the midst of the dust, alone and writhing in the heat, eight miles from the Mediterranean coast' (INT, 4).

The doctrine of intentionality is crucial because it firmly and unequivocally commits Sartre to the view of direct realism, over against for example, Descartes who, as we saw, doubted the existence (and reality) of the external world as a first step towards acquiring indubitable knowledge. All too often Sartre has been wrongly interpreted as a kind of Cartesian idealist (the view that our ideas represent or reflect the reality of the world, the existence of which may only be confirmed by appealing to the ideas we have of it), so it is important to see here that, from the first, Sartre is committed to realism (the view that the world and its objects exist independently of our ideas of them and that we are immediately and directly aware of their existence). As we have seen, Sartre was also uncomfortable with what he took to be idealist tendencies in the thought of Husserl because of the latter's emphasis on describing structures of consciousness at the expense of the world to which consciousness relates. To the extent that Sartre's interpretation of Husserl's philosophy is correct, we may view Sartre's doctrine of intentionality as giving equal attention to the world towards which our conscious activity intends as to conscious activity itself. Later in his life Sartre corroborated his lifelong commitment to realism: '(what) I have tried to do all my life (is) to provide a philosophical foundation for realism' (*Between Existentialism and Marxism*, trans. John Mathews (New York: William Morrow, 1974) [1971]: 36–7).

Sartre went beyond and *against* the teachings of Husserl in claiming that the unity of what we call our 'conscious states' comes from outside of us. Contra Husserl, Sartre maintained that our 'ego' or 'self' is transcendent (not, note, transcendental) or, outside of us, rather than in us. So what makes all of my imaginings, perceptions, fears, joys and dreams mine or, what individuates them within a single conscious awareness that I call mine is constructed through my engagement in the world among others. Sartre argues, then, that our sense of self comes from outside, from the world, from others; the ego is 'outside, in the world, like the ego of another' (Sartre 1957: 31). Hence, and here Sartre is very un-Cartesian, we do not 'find ourselves' or discover our identity by looking inside, or by way of some kind of meditative introspection; rather, we discover who we are through the mediation of other people as we appear before them. Thus Sartre notes that Descartes improperly privileged reflection over concious activity in identifying consciousness with reflection, which can only be a secondary mode of our conscious activity, leading him to remark, 'The consciousness which says *I Think* is precisely not the consciousness which thinks' (Sartre 1957: 45). There is, contrary to Husserl, then, no transcendental ego lurking behind or hiding deep within us that directs our conscious acts. In point of fact, Sartre charges, Husserl contradicts his own phenomenological method in giving the transcendental ego, an entity we do not encounter in our datum of experience, pride of place in his philosophy. And why assume an entity's existence to explain what we actually do experience? In a radical move away from Husserl, then, Sartre insists that the unity of all of our conscious activity resides on one side of the equation: in the world among others; we need not assume anything more and, indeed, it would be incorrect phenomenological procedure to attempt to assume more because we do not have access to, or direct experience of, any such transcendental, hidden subterranean 'I'.

We might wonder why an ego has been so readily assumed by philosophers, and certainly not only philosophers; the entire theoretical underpinnings of psychoanalysis depend on the existence of not only the unconscious, which Sartre also denies, but the ego as well. Sartre's reply is that we have constructed the ego as a stable placeholder for the 'self' in order to hide the fact of our own freedom. Our confrontation with our freedom is very often experienced in what Sartre calls anguish because we are afraid to change our lives. It is thus much easier to think of oneself as unable to change, as not free to change, with an identity as solid and stable as a rock. But, we have seen that on Sartre's account the principle of identity that applies to rocks, tables and other objects cannot apply to persons precisely because Sartre's phenomenological ontology has shown that persons are freely able to be *other* than what they are in virtue of their conscious awareness and activity. Thus even though I may have a temper, I am not my anger. Even though I feel myself to be rather shy, I am not my shyness. No matter how hard I try, I will never be able to have a fixed essence or identity for the simple reason that it is impossible to fix or hold in place what is a free movement towards a future of possibilities. As we will see, the tendency of persons is to do just this, to deny their freedom and to hold or fix themselves, as though suspended in motion or frozen in time. This is what Sartre calls self-deception or bad faith, and the construction of the ego is one strategy that has been invoked to deny our freedom:

Perhaps, in reality, the essential function of the ego is not so much theoretical as practical ... (P)erhaps the essential role of the ego is to mask from consciousness its very spontaneity ... Everything happens ... as if consciousness constituted the ego as a false representation of itself, as if consciousness hypnotized itself before this ego which it has constituted, absorbing itself in the ego as if to make the ego its guardian and its law ... (Sartre 1957: 100–1)

Because our conscious activity has been shown to be immediately and in the first instance intentional activity, relating to a world outside of us, Sartre claims that we are always implicitly aware of ourselves as free. He surmises that the ego's central role is to construct a stable, fixed self that masks the spontaneous movement of our conscious activity and tries to pin our conscious activity down. Our motivation to deny our freedom in bad faith is a fear of our own freedom, or a sense of anguish before our freedom. We will later see how bad faith is possible and why it is 'bad'. For now it is sufficient to point out that the transcendental ego has been shown to be a false construct, but useful to the bad faith project of denying one's own freedom.

One of the interesting consequences of Sartre's claim that the ego is transcendent is that it implies that we have a more intimate awareness of ourselves, but not a genuine or more objective understanding of ourselves than we have of others: 'My I, in effect, is *no more certain for consciousness than the I of other men*. It is only more intimate' (Sartre 1957: 104). We will see later how this claim bears importantly on Sartre's view of authentic interpersonal relations. For now it will be sufficient to point out that Sartre's claim that the ego is in the world among other egos is significant because it suggests that we first absorb what is given to us in the world through our interactions with other people; our 'personality' or 'character' is a construction or creation of our social encounters in the world. Sartre fully develops this view in *BN* and in his plays and novels as well; through the gaze of the other, my identity can be fixed or frozen in such a way as to limit or promote my freedom. The other confers on me a stable and coherent sense of self; she gives me an 'essence' that may either help or hurt me. The view that the ego is first in the world among other egos also suggests that we are not privileged with respect to our sense of self; our sense of self may be *closer* to us because it is ours, but it is not thereby more objectively known by us.[3] Hence, on Sartre's view, we first come to know about ourselves through our interaction with others who act like our mirror.[4] Thus for Sartre, the self is, in the first instance, a social self.

v. AWARENESS AND REFLECTION

In *BN*, Sartre continues to explore the meaning of self-awareness, especially in relation to freedom: what does it mean to be aware of ourselves and experience ourselves as intentional beings? Specifically, he offers a distinction between what he calls pre-reflective and reflective awareness that plays a crucial role in his account of human freedom. An example will help to illustrate this distinction: If I am playing a game of tennis, reading a novel or engrossed in a conversation with someone I am not directly or reflectively aware of myself, but I am rather aware of the activities with which I am engaged (the serve of the tennis ball, the plot of the novel, what is being said in my conversation and how I will respond, and so on). Because I am completely engaged and absorbed in an activity, I am not immediately or reflectively aware of my 'I' or 'self'; rather, I have only an implicit, indirect, or pre-reflective awareness of my 'I' or 'self'. Thus, I never can quite 'catch myself' in the act itself since I am absorbed not in myself, but in what I am doing (playing tennis, reading a novel, having a conversation). But now suppose someone suddenly interrupts my activity and asks, 'What are you doing?' At this juncture my awareness shifts and I become *reflectively* aware of myself as engaging in this activity by replying, 'I am playing tennis'; or 'I am reading a novel'; or 'I am having a conversation.' This distinction shows, once again, that my awareness of myself comes from my activity in the world, and that this awareness is a consequence of my interaction with the world, rather than a starting point of reflection (and here Sartre is radically opposed to Descartes for whom the 'I' is a starting point of reflection). Our sense of self for Sartre truly emerges only in action, not in reflection. Sartre thus notes that we exist not as an ego, but rather as a 'presence to ourselves':

> Thus from its first arising, consciousness by the pure nihilating movement of reflection makes itself personal, for what confers personal existence on a being is not the possession of an Ego—which is only *the sign* of the personality—but it is the fact that the being exists for itself as a presence to itself. (Sartre 1956: 103)

To summarize briefly, then, in pre-reflective awareness I am only pre-reflectively aware of my 'I' because I am completely absorbed in an activity and all of my focus is on that activity (a conversation I am engaged in, for example). With respect to the issue of our freedom, we are always aware of our freedom, Sartre claims, pre-reflectively which is how, we will see, it is possible to deny our freedom. In reflective awareness my 'I' appears when I am moment-arily interrupted and my sense of myself suddenly shifts from a pre-reflective to a reflective mode. This is the awareness that appears, notes Sartre, 'when we cease our activities and attempt to discover what our activities mean' (Sartre 1956: 103).

First introduced in *TE* and later fully developed in his post-humously published *Notebooks for an Ethics* (hereafter '*Note-books*') is yet a third kind of reflection, namely, pure reflection, of which we will have more to say in the next chapter. For now we will simply point out that in pure reflection there is a momentary aware-ness of ourselves as agents engaged in an activity while not ceasing in that activity or 'turning that activity into an object of study' (Sartre 1956: 103). In pure reflection I question myself even while I am engaged in an activity, and such questioning involves an acute awareness of my freedom. Rather than attempt (in bad faith) to 'find myself' and pin down the 'real me' in reflection, or reflect excessively upon myself as an object, I become, in pure reflection, momentarily aware of the *meaning* of my activity, and hence, of my freedom. Pure reflection is critical to Sartre's account of authen-ticity and authentic relations with others, which we will consider in the next chapter. As a prelude, though, in pure reflection I do not distract myself from the deepest meaning of my past and present actions, or from the fact that my future could be very different. In pure reflection I become acutely aware that my global choice of myself, what Sartre calls my fundamental project, can change.

vi. OUR FUNDAMENTAL PROJECT

While we have seen that for Sartre there is no transcendental ego lying behind or within our conscious activity, there is, he thinks, a 'unity of the self' or, a 'fundamental project.' This deep source of agency, he notes, is future oriented, existentially contingent and not conceptually known by us. We make ourselves and define our lives by projecting towards a future and by perpetually going beyond the situation in which we find ourselves. All of my desires, beliefs, reasons, convictions and experiences, he states, 'derive their mean-ing from an original projection of myself which stands as my choice of myself and the world' (Sartre 1956: 39).

Our fundamental project designates our original and global choice of ourselves in the world. It is, Sartre says, the 'primary project which is recognized as the project which can no longer be interpreted in terms of any other and which is total' (Sartre 1956: 479). The fundamental project, he notes, is 'what makes all experience possible [and] is ... an original upsurge of the for-itself as presence to the object which it is not (Sartre 1956: 176). Here again we can appreciate both Sartre's dramatic language disclosing conscious activity as an 'upsurge' and his playing with the negative (our presence to the object which we are not). Our fundamental project is 'original' and 'fundamental' in a transcendental sense; that is, it is the very condition of our being in the world ... it is the project which makes all of my other projects possible and under which all other projects may be interpreted. Sartre seems to want to say, then, that the most fundamental relation we have to existence is not one of knowing, or one of reason, or cognitive, all of which may only be secondary, but it is one that these relations themselves depend upon and, moreover, one that makes these relations possible at all. Sartre is speaking about what is fundamentally basic to all human experience, and not to anything particular in that experience. The initial choice of ourselves, then, is our most basic way of being-in-the world; it constitutes our very connection to existence and does not rest on anything more fundamental; we apprehend this choice, Sartre says, 'as not deriving from any prior reality' (Sartre 1956: 464) and it is so fundamental and deep-rooted that it 'does not imply any other meaning, and ... refers only to itself' (Sartre 1956: 457).

Importantly, my fundamental project is holistic: every aspect of our lives expresses a 'thematic organization and an inherent meaning in this totality' (Sartre 1956: 468). Everything we do, even the most seemingly insignificant act, reflects a deeper, original choice of ourselves. Sartre offers the example of the fatigued hiker to illustrate one possible fundamental project. The hiker's tiredness

is given as a way of appropriating the mountain ... and [of] being victor over it. Thus my companion's fatigue is lived in a vaster project of a trusting abandon to nature, of a passion consented to in order that it may exist at full strength, and at the same time the project of sweet mastery and appropriation. It is only in and through this project that the fatigue will be able to be understood and that it will have meaning for him. (Sartre 1956: 587)

In this example, the companion's fatigue is revealing; it reveals something basic and fundamental about him – it reveals his total and original choice of himself in the world. Thus in Sartre's view all of our subsidiary projects reveal, each in their own way, our original choice of ourselves. While Sartre's example shows the companion's fatigue as his choice to abandon himself to nature and gaining mastery over it, suppose someone else chose to give in to her fatigue at the moment she felt 'too tired to go on'. Suppose she decides to simply give up and throw her knapsack on the side of the trail, refusing to continue. This, too, Sartre says, reveals her fundamental, original choice of herself in the world and a whole different set of values present themselves 'giving in to one's fatigue' rather than embracing it as a challenge to be overcome. Suppose, now, that our second hiker decides to resist her fatigue and forge ahead up the mountain. Sartre says of course she may do so, but the important question is, at what cost does she do so? For most of us, the cost is very often too great, and as a result we tend to settle into our fundamental projects as wet cement settles into concrete.

In another illuminating example, Sartre's study of the French poet Jean Genet, the child Genet is branded a thief because he innocently takes something from a bureau drawer. Sartre shows how Genet then chooses to adopt the fundamental project of 'thiefhood': Genet becomes the thief that society needs. Genet's fundamental project was to accept what society made of him, only unlike most of us, his fundamental project is authentic because it is revolutionary: As a poet Genet offers society a glimpse of its own greed and need for evil; he absorbs the unworthy and inferior status society has conferred on him in order to give back what society has created so that society can confront its own need to create an underclass that it depends on to sustain itself.

Our fundamental project reveals 'not my relations with this or that particular object in the world, but my total being-in-the-world' (Sartre 1956: 65). Importantly, we actively construct our project; it is not passively undergone. All of the influences that we might like to think of as causing or determining us in one way or another, affect us not for what they are in themselves, but for what we make of them. We have already appreciated that on Sartre's account, antecedent conditions such as our genetic blueprint and environmental and social factors are in an important sense *chosen* by us because we decide what meaning they will have for us as we *project* ourselves beyond them. What Sartre calls our 'facticity' – those brute 'facts' about us, such as the place, time and circumstances of our birth, our skin colour, our socio-economic status and cultural conditions, can act on us only to the extent that we comprehend them, that is, transform them into a situation: 'The environment can act on the subject only to the exact extent that he comprehends it; that is, transforms it into a situation' (Sartre 1956: 572).

Notwithstanding that we transform what is given to us into a situation, the choice we make of ourselves is not, on Sartre's account, causally vacuous, but takes place against a background of givens. It is up to us to assume them, find meaning in them, and make them significant as a part of our lives. They are there, given, but they do not come ready-made or pre-packaged. To the extent that we make what is given to us into a situation, we surpass that situation. Sartre offers the example of how one may live one's disability by turning it into a situation:

> Even this disability from which I suffer I have assumed by the very fact that I live; I surpass it toward my own project, I make of it the necessary obstacle for my being, and I cannot be crippled without choosing myself as crippled. This means that I choose the way in which I constitute my disability (as "unbearable," "humiliating," "to be revealed to all," "an object of pride," "the justification for my failures," etc.). (Sartre 1956: 328)

Thus, for Sartre the original choice of ourselves is the choice '. . . by which all foundations and all reasons come into being' (Sartre 1956: 479), and it is not itself founded. It is, he says, a kind of groundless ground by which we orient ourselves towards the world; it is a kind of 'contingent foundation' that is fragile and open to change (although, as we have indicated, Sartre maintains that most of us resist changing our fundamental project).

We have seen how our fundamental project is revealed in the ways in which I orient myself towards the world. My acts reveal to the discerning observer a fundamental way in which I relate myself to the world. Importantly, our fundamental project is lived by us, but this does not mean that it is known by us: '. . . if the fundamental project is fully experienced by the subject and hence wholly conscious, that certainly does not mean that it must by the same token be known by him; quite the contrary' (Sartre 1956: 570). Our fundamental project is not necessarily known by us because, as we have seen, reflection on ourselves for Sartre is not privileged; while we indeed have a more intimate awareness of ourselves than we do of others, we do not thereby have a more conceptual awareness. Our first and immediate relation to ourselves and to the world in which we live is not, on Sartre's account, conceptual or reflective; it is pre-reflective and engaged action shooting out towards a world of possibility. And because we learn about ourselves, not through introspection, but through the mediation of others, our relations with others depend, as we will see, on whether the other's appraisal of us confirms or denies our freedom. Sartre's study of Genet is relevant here because he shows how Genet saw himself as others saw him, namely as a thief. Genet accepted his 'thiefhood' by appropriating the value that society conferred on him: he became the thief that society needed, and then surpassed this condition to become a revolutionary poet. But Genet first had to endure what society conferred on him as a result of an innocent childhood act. All too often, Sartre contends, others attempt to deny rather than confirm our freedom and in so doing attempt to 'steal' our freedom from us. The attempt to steal freedom from another is a result, Sartre claims, of the widespread tendency of persons to slip into dishonesty or 'bad faith' concerning the issue of their freedom. Most of us, Sartre thinks, are engaged in the dishonest project of self-completion or fullness, what Sartre ambiguously calls the desire to be God or the *causa sui* (self-cause).

vii. THE DESIRE TO BE NECESSARY

In *BN*, Sartre claims that in most human endeavours and relation-ships we are seeking to escape from our status as merely contingent, factual beings in order to achieve the state of a necessary being which is its own foundation. In the western philosophical tradition, and at least since the thirteenth century in the writings of Saint Thomas Aquinas, the usual English name given for this human longing is 'God'. In Sartre's view, we attempt to achieve Godhood, or what he calls the impossible union of the in-itself-for-itself (alternatively, the *ens causa sui* or self-cause). This project, he says, is pre-reflective in the sense that we live it without directly questioning it. Moreover, it proves to be implicitly dishonest because we cannot but be aware, even if still only implicitly, that we can never be in any final way necessary or a foundation for ourselves. We have seen that for Sartre we are always pre-reflectively aware that we are at a distance from the world because we are free to call the world into question. So, too, we are also pre-reflectively aware that we can never achieve the kind of necessary being or fullness that 'God' would have if 'God' existed. Indeed, if God existed God would be a pure superfluity and overflowing of Being; God would be in need of nothing. And God would certainly not need to question 'Itself' or 'Its' relation with the world. Sartre holds, then, that the desire to be 'God' to achieve a synthesis of necessity and freedom is experienced by us as a value because it is experienced as lacking to our existence, and is hence one that is perpetually sought. This desire is a contradictory, hence impossible, aim – a self-defeating desire because, Sartre notes, 'one cannot both be beyond the need of self-foundation and be responsible for achieving it' (Sartre 1956: xxvii). I want both to be the causing of myself, and yet be already caused. It is not difficult to see that this desire constitutes the alienation of our conscious activity because it involves us in a contradiction that keeps our sense of ourselves divided. Thus rather than our conscious activity being a presence for itself, this desire attempts consciously to found or justify this presence; this is why Sartre describes this attempt in *BN* as futile and dramatically claims that man is a 'useless passion'.

The desire to be necessary is of course a denial of our freedom; it is a project, however, that we freely choose and, Sartre believes, one of the primary ways in which we live and believe in our freedom. Indeed, it is the most common way; however, we want to be careful here because Sartre's view is subtle. He claims that we flee our anguished awareness of our freedom most of the time, not *all* of the time (Sartre 1956: 556). Still, adopting a project to be a necessary being is an example of one of the most typical flights from freedom and the accompanying anguish, and one, we mistakenly believe, precludes us from making choices in a dangerous and uncertain world. In our attempt to pin down or ground freedom, we falsely believe that we thereby give our freedom a secure foundation; but clearly such an effort will always prove impossible because our freedom can never be a foundation. Sartre's ontology finds, then, that our conscious activity cannot appropriate or assimilate Being (what is); like the air that sustains the flight of a bird, our freedom sustains us, without ever weighing us down (unless, however, one is speaking of the anguish we feel in facing the fact of our freedom as a kind of burden). And if one *is* speaking about the anguish that accompanies our freedom, then it would have to be true that many of us experience it as difficult and even frightening. In fact, our anguished awareness of our own freedom can be so terrible, so frightening, so burdensome, that we adopt the desire to achieve impossible necessity as a primary project that will subsume other projects, other attitudes, other ways of being and other modes of existence, all of which Sartre says are adopted in bad faith.

viii. BAD FAITH AND 'GOOD' FAITH AS ATTITUDES TOWARDS OUR FREEDOM

We can see now how Sartre's characterization of our conscious activity as a lack of coincidence of the self with its own selfhood (a person does not exist as a table or chair exist because, unlike objects whose attributes and characteristics are exhausted by what they are, persons may always become more than what they are) and his claim that to be aware does not imply that we have conceptualized that of which we are aware to provide the conditions under which bad faith (*mauvais-foi*) or self-deception is possible. That is, because our being is freedom and negation, we are capable of denying our freedom. Here, we might recall that both negative statements such as 'I am not free to act' or 'I could never change jobs' and the real absence or lack we do find in the world originate from our conscious activity as a *negating* activity. The crucial implication with respect to the possibility of bad faith is that our negative activity also involves our capacity to freely question the meaning of our existence, including whether we are free. When we do question the meaning of our existence, we very often experience deep anxiety or even a kind of nausea that Sartre's character Roquentin experiences when he confronts the roots of the chestnut tree and finds himself utterly contingent or 'de trop' (superfluous). What do we do? Typically, Sartre says, we flee from these uncomfortable feelings and our flight manifests itself in the way we lie to ourselves about our freedom. Just as we saw with the Desire to be Necessary or to be 'God', the attempt to flee from freedom and anguish are pre-reflective projects of freedom. Thus although we are always pre-reflectively aware of the freedom we are trying to hide from ourselves, the project of hiding this freedom may not be known by us; we may successfully lie to ourselves about our projects without this lie being an *object* of reflection or knowledge. This is why bad faith is a *project* of believing in and living our freedom in a certain way: this is why we are able to *believe* the lies we tell ourselves.

One of the ways we can see bad faith in action is in role-playing. When one assumes a particular role in society uncritically, and views that role as emanating from 'nature' or from 'society', one fails to see oneself as the creator and author of the role one has chosen. The professor with his tweed jacket and aloof arrogance, or the patronizing physician whose self-importance undermines the possibility of an authentic doctor–patient relationship, or the woman whose retreat into motherhood precludes her from doing anything else, are all instances in which persons have allowed social roles and expectations to trump their humanity. Sartre offers his own examples, and one cannot help but see the humour in them:

> A grocer who dreams is offensive to the buyer, because such a grocer is not wholly a grocer. Society demands that he limit himself to his function as a grocer, just as a soldier at attention makes himself into a soldier-thing with a direct gaze which does not see at all, which is no longer meant to see, since it is the rule and not the interest of the moment which determines the point he must fix his eyes on (the sight "fixed" at ten paces"). There are indeed many precautions to imprison a man in what he is, as if we lived in perpetual fear that he might escape from it, that he might break away and suddenly elude his condition. (Sartre 1956: 59)[5]

Here we can see the force of Sartre's claim that society expects roles to be filled mechanically and unquestionably and, far too often, we willingly carry out the mandate. To be sure, insofar as we 'accept our lot in life' and adopt social roles as given antecedently, we fail to see ourselves as the free source of our own existence. To live in such a way is to resign ourselves in bad faith; it is to lie to ourselves about the very issue of our freedom. It is, Socrates would say, to live as though we were sleepwalking through our lives, wilfully unaware of the violence such an attitude does to ourselves and to others.

Bad faith may be understood, then, as one of the ways we believe in and live our freedom. Because we have seen that our freedom is always in question, we are able to decide how we believe in and live our freedom; thus our attitudes towards our freedom are attitudes of belief or faith, rather than objective knowledge or certainty. And, just as our other beliefs may be held with or without evidence or support, our beliefs about ourselves can be critical or uncritical. Importantly, since it is the nature of belief that it can only persuade, not convince (because beliefs are not apodictic or certain), we may choose the way in which we face evidence about a particular belief we have. And since our beliefs can never be perfectly justified because they are always in question, we can and often do exploit the fact that a belief can never be perfectly justified. We do this either by not requiring too much evidence since, after all, no amount of evidence will ever convince, or by requiring so much evidence that we refuse to believe anything at all, since we could never have enough evidence to convince us. Thus, in the first case, George W. Bush, Dick Cheney and the CIA forged in bad faith a false belief between Iraq and the events of September 11 that could thereby serve as a pretence for invading Iraq. They did so by lowering the bar of acceptable and persuasive evidence to such an extent to convince the American people that waiting for further evidence to support the invasion would be inconsequential (and even danger-ous, since a delay would pose a further risk to America). Here the belief that Iraq was involved in the events of September 11 becomes virtually perfectly justified (impossible in itself because of the nature of belief) and hence need not be questioned. The second case, where one refuses to believe anything at all on the basis of insufficient evidence (since any amount of evidence can merely persuade, but never convince), is manifested by those who refuse to believe that human practices are in large part responsible for climate change. Notwithstanding the fact that notable scientists from across the globe have weighed in on the reality of climate change and the relationship between human activity and climate change, there are still many people who refuse to believe both the fact of climate change and the cause of it or, alternatively, they believe that cli-mate change is happening, but doubt that humans are in any way responsible for it.

So we see that bad faith concerns our relationship to belief and faith itself; one can exploit the nature of belief by requiring too much evidence or by insisting that one can never have enough evi-dence (so that *any* belief may be justified). One may, of course, also fudge evidence to convince oneself (and others) that the evidence they have is persuasive or not. And when bad faith requires that a belief be perfectly justified, the more common manoeuvre, we can adduce any kind of evidence for our beliefs; at this moment, Sartre notes, a peculiar kind of evidence appears, namely non-persuasive evidence (Sartre 1956: 68). We see, then, that the relationship between bad faith and freedom concerns the very issue of how we live our freedom. How do we live our freedom? Do we hide it or flee from it, or do we face it? What kind of attitude do we adopt in the face of our freedom?

If we face our freedom critically rather than uncritically our attitude may be understood as one of 'good' faith. While bad faith notices and apprehends (persuasive) evidence, it does not allow itself to be persuaded by this evidence (so no amount of evidence contrary to the Bush Administration's scheme of invading Iraq would have convinced them to reconsider); it does not allow itself to be persuaded and transformed into good faith. 'Good faith' looks critically at evidence and allows itself to be persuaded accordingly; it allows itself to be critical and open rather than closed and uncritical. It accepts that all beliefs are in question, but not so much that no evidence at all could possibly persuade us or not so much that we can make *any* kind of evidence count as persuasive.[6]

ix. BAD FAITH, GOOD FAITH AND OUR FUNDAMENTAL PROJECT

We have seen how our awareness of our freedom is always, necessarily, unstable because freedom is itself always in question. Good faith allows us to confront the way in which we view the possibility of altering our fundamental project: we may keep the possibility remote, or we may face it squarely. We have all known people, perhaps even ourselves, who have felt themselves to be in 'a rut'. Some people believe themselves to be so hopelessly beyond the possibility of extricating themselves from their 'rut' that they convince themselves that no other options or opportunities are possible; it is as though they are sinking slowly in quicksand or have their feet stuck in rapidly drying cement. We can see the extent to which these people are denying their freedom in bad faith. But it is important to see that these statements of being unable to change are manifestations of a more fundamental attitude or project in bad faith that serve to confirm it: the project to be a necessary, confined being, no different from a rock or a table. Sartre notes that when we deliberate, the chips are down, and what he means by this is that all of my deliberations take place well within my overall project; we face the real issue of our freedom when we acknowledge the possibility of changing the project itself. An example will be helpful here. I met a mathematician and computational models analyst for a large corporation in New York. He is Chilean but has been living in New York now for several years, and is considering pursuing his doctorate in mathematics. But he has had a nagging feeling, at first infrequent and incoherent, but now frequent and concrete, that he is selling his soul to corporate America. He feels stuck, sitting behind a desk all day long five days a week working for people who only care if he is able to make a profit for the company. He has been feeling increasingly isolated and alone, and his sense of himself divided and fragmented. He mentioned his dream of returning to Chile to cultivate a vineyard in the country and wondered out loud if he could ever do it. It would mean engaging in a business venture that would be uncertain and, as he said, 'I could lose everything . . . all that I have worked for.' What should he do? We know what Sartre would say. He could, despite all the perceived risk and uncertainty, forge ahead with his dream. He could give up his life in New York, his profession, his financial security – all of it. The important question for him, according to Sartre, is *at what price* does he do this: 'Doubtless I could have done otherwise, but at what price? . . . it becomes evident that the act could not have been modified without at the same time supposing a fundamental modification of my original choice of myself' (Sartre 1956: 464).

Importantly, one does not change one's fundamental project in a vacuum. Changing one's project, which Sartre sometimes refers to as 'conversion', takes place against a background of the past: 'A converted atheist is not simply a believer; he is a believer who has made past within himself the project of being an atheist' (Sartre 1956: 466–7). At this juncture I don't know what my friend will decide. But he is looking at his life, Sartre would say, with a critical awareness that the choices he makes will inscribe certain values in the world by which he can live. He is recognizing the possibility of a different kind of life with a different set of values. In good faith we accept the challenge of our freedom. We accept the ambiguity and tension of our 'troubled' freedom, for our freedom is always in question. In bad faith, as we have seen, we tend to deny the challenge of our freedom and adopt a particular lifestyle that allows us to live our lives in complacency and resignation. Our bad faith attitude prompts us to say, 'Let others do what I cannot or will not do.' Or, 'What good could I possibly do?' In bad faith we do not ask more from ourselves; we merely live out the life we have. In bad faith we think of ourselves as already made; we label ourselves as 'lazy', 'sad', 'depressed' or 'angry' and become thereby as impenetrable as a stone, as helpless and hopeless as a bird with a broken wing. And like the bird with a broken wing that cannot be repaired, we think these labels attach to us, belong to us irrevocably; they will be with us forever and will serve to define us once and for all. We cannot, we think, move beyond them.

Bad faith affects, of course, not only the individual, but also those with whom the individual has intimate or social relations. In this sense, bad and good faith may be distinguished by the ways in which we experience our relationship with others. From this perspective we may regard them, as Sartre does, as having a moral or ethical dimension.

CHAPTER 5

RELATIONS WITH OTHERS AND AUTHENTIC EXISTENCE

Before you come alive, life is nothing; it's up to you to give it a meaning, and value is nothing else but the meaning that you choose. In that way, you see, there is a possibility of creating a human community.

(Sartre 1998: 49)

i. RELATIONS WITH OTHERS

Sartre's claim in *BN* that conflict marks our original relation with other people, and his dramatic statement in his play, *No Exit*, that 'hell is other people' (Sartre 1976: 47) have been the focus of much debate about the possibility of genuine, authentic relations with others. In *BN* the chapter entitled 'Concrete Relations with Others'[1] Sartre claims that ontologically, 'The Look' leads to a series of objectifications, and in consequence the conflict of freedom arises. Suppose, Sartre says, that I am peering through a keyhole and suddenly become aware of someone watching me. At this moment, the comfort of my solitude has been disrupted and I feel ashamed under the look of the other. Under the Other's gaze, then, I see myself as shameful or stupid, and I attempt to escape from this appraisal (from the look which reveals to me that I am shameful or stupid) by making the Other into an object. But of course I will not be successful in doing this because the Other, as freedom, cannot be turned into an object. Still, my attempt to do so, and the Other's attempt to do the same to me in order to reclaim her subjectivity under my objectifying gaze leads to the kind of original conflict Sartre sees in human relationships. Sartre claims conflict is necessary because my attempt to reclaim myself as I want to be and as I think I am will involve a bad faith (bad faith because dishonest) attempt to degrade the Other's revelation of me by objectifying her. Recall that Sartre claims as early as *TE* that we owe our very exteriority to the Other; that is, we come to know about ourselves primarily through the mediation and appraisal of the Other. If the Other is in bad faith, or has, as Sartre's ontology has found most of us to have, a fundamental project to deny our freedom and achieve necessary being, the Other's appraisal of me can be damaging and false because it may attempt to limit or deny my free subjectivity by freezing me into a thing.

In everyday human life we can see how bad faith projects play out in the world. We have seen that for Sartre the Other, in wanting to be the foundation of his own existence, and in wanting to appropriate Being, 'steals my freedom from me', and threatens to turn me into an object. For example, one can readily see how subsidiary bad faith projects are manifested in race relations. Because of ongoing, longstanding and deeply rooted institutional and social racism, the black person's freedom is 'stolen' from her by white people who, through active or insidious practices sustain those policies that maintain social, economic and educational injustice and inequality. In Sartre's view, racism is a secondary bad faith structure of society and is so pernicious that it is possible for an individual to slowly take in and appropriate as one's own the racist attitudes in their society. This is particularly true if one lacks a sense of self that takes freedom as a fundamental value since, as we have seen, one's sense of self is forever vulnerable and fragile in the face of the Other. It might be wondered what makes the bad faith attitude of racism 'bad', other than the mere fact that Sartre deplores it. Importantly, the issue for Sartre is not to say that we are 'bad' in the sense of 'evil' or that we are bad in the sense that we have a corrupt human nature. He is clearly not suggesting that we are 'bad' or 'evil' by nature for the simple reason that he denies that there can be such a thing as 'human nature' in this sense. Sartre's commitment to freedom blocks both essentialism and reductionism of any kind, e.g., that we are essentially thus and so have an 'essential human nature' or that our human condition may be reduced to the tendency to behave badly or to always be tempted to do bad things. And Sartre is not claiming, as we will see in the next chapter especially, that bad faith is 'bad' because it violates some kind of absolute or objective moral principle. The real issue, it seems, is whether persons are willing to make the effort to live their lives freely and uncritically, that is, whether they are willing to become authentic. Thus the racist's attitude can be said to be 'bad' on Sartre's account precisely because she denies freedom and lives her life uncritically. She does this by viewing others as naturally 'stupid', 'lazy' or 'criminal'. These labels limit the humanity of others from the outset by seriously impeding their process of becoming; if one's sense of self has already been decided by others, then in what sense can one genuinely become or, to use Sartre's language, live their freedom? The racist, then, denies what is most important and true about our humanity, namely, that we are all projects-in-the-world aiming towards a certain kind of future. In ascribing fixed characteristics, qualities and properties to others, the racist denies that we are all projects-in-the-making who lack absolute identity with ourselves: the Other is not stupid or lazy as the table is round or flat. Suppose, though, that one pushes Sartre on this and claims that one may 'freely' choose racism as a bad faith project of limiting the freedom of others one deems to be inferior. As we will see in the next chapter, Sartre's commitment to freedom precludes him from invoking antecedent moral laws, principles, injunctions or mandates that could serve as commandments against practices that deny the freedom of others. But what Sartre does appeal to is the possibility of one becoming authentic by choosing and sustaining a project that promotes, rather than denies, the freedom of others. The point is that if we are authentic, the road to racism is closed because authenticity recognizes that others exist equally with us in the world.

In *Anti-Semite and Jew* (1946), Sartre describes the anti-Semite as a person who is in the thick of self-deception. In depicting anti-Semitism as bad faith, Sartre wishes to show that the anti-Semite is deeply self-deceptive about his own and the other's freedom; he shows, through the fear and anxiety of the anti-Semite, how we need to see others as naturally evil and less than human in order for us to feel human. In viewing the other as less than human, I then view myself as possessing a justified humanity, and I keep the possibility of questioning myself, my relation to others and to the world at a safe distance; I remain uncritical and closed. If we recall our earlier example regarding the bad faith of the Bush Administration's decision to invade Iraq, we can readily see how important it became for the Administration to demonize to the American people the Iraqis as 'terrorists' and Iraq as a 'failed state' that harbours terrorists. The rhetoric of duality in slogans, such as 'good versus evil' and 'us versus them', was captured in the inflammatory statement George W. Bush issued in his State of the Union Address, 'You're either with us or against us'.

The persistence of the original bad faith project, wherein one does not see oneself as just one person in the world among others, and as the source through which meaning and value come into the world, naturally gives rise to secondary projects which are equally in bad faith. We have seen that racism is just one example of a secondary bad faith project. Sexism and classism are other ways of being in the world that attempt to degrade in bad faith the humanity of the other. Importantly, in limiting another's freedom one reveals one's fundamental attitude towards oneself, others and the world. Thus in all forms of racism there is a free project aimed at limiting the humanity of a particular race; in all forms of sexism there is a free project aimed at limiting the humanity of women;[2] in all forms of classism there is a free project aimed at limiting the humanity of the underclass and the working poor. And because we owe our very exteriority to the look of the other, Sartre notes that 'We must recognize here that we have encountered a real limit to our freedom – that is, a way of being which is imposed on us without our freedom being its foundation' (1956: 524). By this Sartre means, whether Jew, woman or working poor, the person in bad faith over-determines their object of derision to such an extent that Jew, woman and working poor cannot escape this over-determination because they cannot avoid the way others see and objectify them. And yet, they must nonetheless respond to their situation in some way.

If, however, the Other is in 'good' faith and has adopted freedom as a fundamental value, cooperation is not only possible, but actively sought. Indeed, Sartre recognized, also as early as *TE*, that our willed 'conversion' to authenticity through what he calls 'pure reflection', involves a renunciation of the desire to be a necessary being and a pursuit of values that confirm and validate my own and others' freedom. But it is important to note that this cooperation is not given in advance. Here, Sartre distances himself from Heidegger, who views cooperation among persons as ontologically basic, and hence, guaranteed in the form of what Heidegger refers to as 'Mitsein' or Being-With. On the contrary, for Sartre the basic ontological fact with which we are confronted is not the 'we', it is the 'you and the me'. What Sartre wishes to emphasize is that it is *we* who, through our individual and collective efforts, and through our choices and actions, create the very conditions for cooperation or conflict. Indeed, this is why bad faith is not *merely* a theoretical attitude, but a *project* of believing in, and actually living our freedom; even the self-styled contemplative is doing something in the world. If cooperation is not guaranteed in advance and we must create the very conditions that make it possible how, on Sartre's account, may we do so?

ii. EMBRACING FREEDOM AS THE SOURCE OF VALUES

At the end of *BN* Sartre asks a series a provocative questions that he says will be devoted to a future work on ethics:

> What will become of freedom if it turns its back upon this (transcendent) value? Will freedom carry this value along with it whatever it does and even in its very turning back upon the in-itself-for-itself? Or will freedom by the very fact that it apprehends itself as freedom in relation to itself, be able to put an end to the reign of this value? In particular, is it possible for freedom to take itself for a value as the source of all value, or must it necessarily be defined in relation to a transcendent value which haunts it? And in case it could will itself as its own possible and its determining value, what would this mean? (Sartre 1957: 627)[3]

Sartre replies to these and other questions in his posthumously published,[4] unfinished *Notebooks for an Ethics*, a compilation of notes written in 1947–1948 on the moral implications of his phenomenological ontology. Specifically, Sartre addresses the possibility of renouncing the original project of the desire to be God (or a necessary being), and suggests that in turning away from this project we will abandon those secondary bad faith projects that animate us in our lives. To relinquish this original project, along with secondary projects, amounts to what Sartre refers to as a 'conversion' to authenticity. The conversion to authenticity is crucial to the very possibility of a Sartrean ethics, and one of his primary aims in *Notebooks* is to show how the idea of conversion to authenticity may be contrasted with the project to be necessary or already 'founded'. Sartre claims that our conversion is prompted by a new desire, namely, a desire to renounce the project of identity and appropriation (the desire that underlies the denial of my freedom) which has revealed itself to be both self-contradictory (a lie) and freely chosen. Our conversion is prompted by a new kind of reflection, what Sartre calls 'pure reflection' that discloses our freedom. In *Notebooks* Sartre refers to 'unveiling' the truth of our project as free: 'The he one meaningful project is that of acting on a concrete situation and modifying it in some way [because] what is necessary has to be done ... authenticity consists in refusing any quest for being, because I am always *nothing*' (Sartre 1992: 475). To refuse to appropriate my being (to make myself necessary) for Sartre is to be prompted by a new kind of reflection to unveil myself as perpetual calling into question the meaning of my existence in relation to others and to the world. Hence, through this new kind of reflection, my existence appears to itself as a question; it does not identify itself with itself. This 'unveiling act' creates, he says, a kind of 'existential vertigo' which occurs when 'the project appears to reflection in its absolute gratuity. Hence it is the human project understood as 'gratuitous at its core and consecrated by a reflective reprise, that makes it into *authentic* existence' (Sartre 1992: 481). To assume our existence as freedom is to assume our gratuity and vulnerability in the face of a dangerous and uncertain world. To assume gratuity at the heart of our project is for Sartre to genuinely commit oneself to an adventure and transform one's contingency into a passion (Sartre 1992: 482): 'We arrive at a type of intuition that will unveil authentic existence: an absolute contingency that has only itself to justify itself by assuming itself and that can assume itself only within itself ... and that justifies itself only by risking losing itself' (Sartre 1992: 482). We are, in Sartre's view, the 'absolute contingency' who must justify ourselves by assuming ourselves as lacking justification. And to assume ourselves reflectively as the gratuitous freedom we are constitutes a conversion that Sartre says 'unveils' and renounces the project to pin down our existence and, at the same time, he notes, 'it realizes a type of unity peculiar to the existent, which is an ethical unity brought about by calling things into question and a contractual agreement with oneself' (Sartre 1992: 479). Moreover, conversion, as the means by which I renounce the 'category of appropriation', introduces a new relation with myself and others, namely, a relation of solidarity; in relinquishing my desire to appropriate myself or others, I will a new relation of solidarity in myself, or 'being with', that will solicit a new relation with others as I seek to promote rather than limit their freedom.

Notice that the way in which we disclose and reveal ourselves, others, and the world is through the process of negation, introduced in Chapter 4. Authentic existence necessarily requires that I assume myself as a lack in order that there might be being. Our consciousness activity, as free, nihilating activity reveals and discloses being by making itself a lack:

> Hence freedom is founding: through it, the world exists; if it nihilates itself, Being is opened into Nothingness. And every possibility of freedom (technological, artistic, etc.) being at the same time an unveiling of Being, manifesting Being. For it is not in passive contemplation that the For-itself makes the most being appear, but on the contrary, through the multiple facets of action. (Sartre 1992: 484)

Here, Sartre is emphasizing that our conscious activity is a project of unveiling that which is not, and that human reality exists as the unveiling of being that gives or carves out meaning in the world (the doctrine of intentionality Sartre borrows from Husserl). Also related to the process of negation is Sartre's claim that one of the conditions for authentic existence is 'to make oneself a lack so that being might be there' (Sartre 1992: 448–9; 514–5). de Beauvoir, whose influence on Sartre was extensive, is clearer than Sartre in her interpretation of him on the issue of 'making oneself a lack':

> Man, Sartre tells us, is 'a being who *makes himself* a lack of being *in order that there might be* being'. The term *in order that* clearly indicates an intentionality. It is not in vain that man nullifies Being. Thanks to him, being is disclosed and he desires this disclosure. There is an original type of attachment to being which is not the relationship 'wanting to be' but rather 'wanting to disclose being'. Now here there is not failure, but rather success. By uprooting himself from the world man makes himself present to the world and makes the world present to him ... Man in his vain attempt to be God, makes himself exist as man ... it is not granted him to exist without tending toward this being which he will never be. But it is possible for him to want

this tension even with the failure it involves. His being is a lack of being, but his lack has a way of being which is precisely existence. (de Beauvoir 1991: 12–13)

Here, de Beauvoir captures the ambiguity of our existence, of our wanting, on the one hand, to pin being down and exist once and for all (as a stone or rock exists, for example) and of our wanting to disclose being (the world and others). Making ourselves a lack of being, she says, is precisely to exist as the freedom we are. To the extent, de Beauvoir notes, that we lose ourselves by agreeing never to regain ourselves, we authentically exist as the freedom we are: 'To attain his truth, man must not attempt to dispel the ambiguity of his being, but on the contrary, accept the task of realizing it. He rejoins himself only to the extent that he agrees to remain at a distance from himself' (de Beauvoir 1991: 113). Hence the world becomes meaningful by our presence in it and, moreover, such a meaningful world will now be lived authentically in a world with others, where the 'other is my concern'. In this sense, both Sartre and de Beauvoir claim that to unveil or disclose is also to create and this creation may be accompanied by joy. As Sartre puts it:

For it is not in passive contemplation that the For-itself makes the most being appear, but on the contrary through the multiple facets of action (Saint-Exupéry). Here joy comes from this curious reality: in creating (governing) the airplane one unveils an aspect of Being that was but was not (since it was for no one, it was in absolute indifference). (Sartre 1992: 485)[5]

To be authentic is to grasp oneself in one's 'deepest structure as creative' (Sartre 1992: 514–5). In authenticity we unveil ourselves as 'condemned to create' (Sartre 1992: 515). Hence authentic existence realizes that it is generous before the world: its 'springing up is the creation of the world' (Sartre 1992: 499). Inauthentic existence, we have seen, is tempted by and maintains the project of being the ultimate foundation of itself. Since it fails to realize in action that it can never found itself once and for all, its repeated efforts to do so often result in an unhappy, and even tragic life: since 'consciousness as nothingness cannot produce Being' (Sartre 1992: 535), this project will always fail. And insofar as we give in to this temptation, we pursue the project in bad faith. We have already seen examples of bad faith and noted Sartre's analysis of it in *BN*. What is missing, however, in *BN*, and what *Notebooks* does offer, is an account of authentic unveiling in contrast to the bad faith appropriation of Being. We have seen that through the project of reflective unveiling, we may embrace ourselves as the gratuitous and troubled freedom we are. We may accept our own contingency as an assumed 'foundationless foundation' and convert to authenticity through *reflective* unveiling. Let us turn in the next section to that special kind of reflection that is new, and that prompts or solicits in us a new kind of awareness of ourselves as free.

iii. 'IMPURE' AND 'PURE' REFLECTION

We have noted that Sartre's ontology posed a difficulty because it demonstrates that the fundamental project or desire of human reality is to achieve 'Godhood', or become a necessary being, yet still be free (what Sartre calls the 'impossible synthesis of the in-itself-for-itself'). That is, as human reality is radically contingent, it desires to achieve necessity and thereby escape the burden of having to make itself. This goal is impossible because in Sartre's view human reality is characterized precisely by the fact that it is never complete, necessary or in possession of an 'essence' or human nature, but is always in-the-making in its projection towards goals that are outside of it.

We also noted that at the end of *BN* Sartre mentions the possibility of putting 'an end to the reign' of the desire to achieve Godhood by choosing a different way of being-in-the-world:

> In particular will freedom by taking itself for an end escape all situation? Or on the contrary, will it remain situated? Or will it situate itself so much the more precisely and the more individually as it projects itself further in anguish as a conditioned freedom and accepts more fully its responsibility as an existent by whom the world comes into being . . . Will freedom, by the very fact that it apprehends itself as freedom in relation to itself, be able to put an end to the reign of this value? (Sartre 1957: 627–8)

At this juncture, however, there appears to be a difficulty. In *BN* Sartre claims that human beings *must* seek Godhood as their ultimate goal and value. This goal, he says, is the ultimate value of our fundamental project. How, then, are we to understand the questions Sartre asks at the end of *BN* that imply that we can turn away from the 'reign' of this value and adopt an authentic attitude instead? Since *BN* addresses ontology and not ethics, Sartre states that he will indeed address these questions in a future work that, we know, was published posthumously as *Notebooks for an Ethics*. That said, in *BN* Sartre does bring our attention to a very important distinction between our pre-reflective and reflective awareness of values (Sartre 1956: 94–5). After telling us that our supreme value is to achieve Godhood, Sartre points out that this value is most often lived pre-reflectively. That is, like other values, we take this value as 'given', and so beyond question; we take this and other values as given in order to avoid the anguish that would result from facing the fact that our freedom alone is their cause. Importantly, these pre-reflective values are to be distinguished from the values that reflection grasps. Sartre says, for example, that 'in [pure] reflection I remain free to direct my attention on these pre-reflective values, or to neglect them' (Sartre 1956: 95). Nothing more is said about this in *BN*, except in the last pages where Sartre briefly mentions the need for a special kind of reflection, namely, pure reflection, which he promises to discuss in detail in a future work on ethics.

But from what little Sartre has said in *BN*, one can still 'catch a glimpse' of what he means by pure reflection, in contrast to impure reflection. It appears that the job of pure reflection would be to call into question and repudiate those values that are lived pre-reflectively, and to 'decide' or 'will' not to value the impossible goal of achieving necessary being (or 'Godhood') that we seek on the *pre-reflective* level. Even though this pre-reflective goal will always remain a value for us *ontologically*, because our very being is troubled in that it is incomplete and in question, we need not adopt or will it as ours. That is, once we recognize that this primary ontological value is not absolutely imposed on us, but comes from the very freedom we are evading, we may 'turn our backs' on this value and 'put an end to its reign'. In *BN*, then, Sartre distinguishes between values that are pre-reflectively sought and those that are reflectively chosen; he does not pursue a discussion of values that are reflectively chosen in *BN* since, he says, it 'is an ontology before conversion' (Sartre 1992: 4).

It is often overlooked that Sartre first introduced the ideas of impure and pure reflection in *Transcendence of Ego*, a work we noted that was inspired by Husserl. There, he provocatively states that pure reflection may provide a 'philosophical foundation for an ethics' (Sartre 1957: 106). Since pure reflection is one of the central concepts he introduces to demonstrate the moral implications of the ontological investigation he carried out in *BN*, we need to appreciate the importance of his discussion of it in *TE*.

iv. PURE REFLECTION AS A 'FOUNDATION FOR AN ETHICS'

In *TE* Sartre criticizes those who reproach phenomenology for being an idealism, that is, 'for drowning reality in the stream of ideas . . . On the contrary, for centuries we have not felt in philosophy so realistic a current. The phenomenologists have plunged man back into the world' (Sartre 1957: 104–5). And in his essay 'Intentionality', Sartre contrasts the 'digestive' philosophy that maintains that all objects of experience are 'contents of consciousness' with Husserl's phenomenology that maintains that conscious activity is outside in the world among other things. He says, for example, 'It is not in some hiding-place that we discover ourselves; it is on the road, in the city, in the midst of the crowd, a thing among things, a man among men.'[6] This, of course, is a familiar idea since we have already noted Sartre's endorsement of Husserl's doctrine of intentionality and the implications this doctrine has for Sartre's emphasis on the *relation* between our conscious activity and the world: we always intend a world outside of us and thereby confer meaning on it.

The significance that *TE* and Sartre's essay on 'Intentionality' has for ethics is that Sartre rejects any philosophical view that would isolate or detach persons from the world by imprisoning them in their own private experiences or internal mental states. Here, Sartre's views are to be distinguished from those of Descartes who, as we have seen, claims that the proper philosophical method by which we may achieve certainty requires that we detach ourselves from the world through meditative introspection and doubt and, moreover, that we discover ourselves in self-reflection, not in a world of others. Sartre's phenomenological commitments preclude the very possibility that the existence of the external world could ever be doubted since our experience proves that we are, in the first instance, always a part of the world in which we live. Thus any sceptical doubts concerning this immediate datum of experience would be regarded as without merit. Further, Sartre's endorsement of Husserl's view that all of our awareness is an awareness of something means that our entire reality as persons is to be related to a world. All content is therefore on the side of objects; there is nothing 'in' our awareness. As we have seen, our awareness possesses no ego, or substantial like 'I' at the origin of its actions; my 'I' is discovered in the world through the mediation of others. Our awareness does not possess states of love or hate, or qualities (being depressed or happy). The me (*moi*), with its states, actions and qualities is just an object among other objects in the world since, for Sartre, what is peculiar to us as persons is that we may always take ourselves as objects, which is to say we may always reflectively ask what it means to be a person in the world among others. One of the most critical points Sartre makes in *TE* is that the relation between the 'me' and the world is one of *interdependency*. And it is precisely through the idea of the interdependency between persons and the world that Sartre understood his philosophy establishes some sort of foundation for an ethics:

> . . . the relation of interdependence established by this absolute consciousness between the me and the World is sufficient for the me to appear as "endangered" before the World, for the me (indirectly) and through the intermediary of states to draw the whole of its content from the World. No more is needed in the way of a philosophical foundation for an ethics and a politics which are absolutely positive. (Sartre 1957: 106)

In *TE* Sartre states that there are two reflections, namely, impure and pure reflection: '. . . the one, impure and conniving, which effects then and there a passage to the infinite (in terms of conceiving of the self as a static object which one was, is, and will be) . . . and the other pure, merely descriptive, which disarms the unreflected consciousness by granting its instantaneousness' (Sartre 1957: 64–5). Moreover, as we have noted, he claims that pure reflection is necessary for a realistic and positive ethics. How, exactly, does Sartre contrast pure reflection with impure reflection? In impure reflection, we construct the ego as possessing a thing-like structure in order to hide the fact that our conscious activity is spontaneous, and so free. Hence Sartre suggests that 'perhaps the essential role of the ego is to mask from consciousness its very spontaneity' (Sartre 1957:

9, 11). That is, the point of constructing the ego may be to give us a sense of substantiality and fullness with respect to our future; it helps us to feel secure and protected in the sense that we think that we do not have to decide the meaning of our own existence. When we constitute the ego as a substantial self, we thereby persuade ourselves that we can escape from our freedom and anguish.

Borrowing from Husserl once again, Sartre refers to impure reflection as the 'natural' attitude, which suggests that it is the normal or usual condition of our conscious activity. In Husserl's phenomenological investigation he temporarily suspends, by way of the 'epoche' or 'phenomenological reduction' questions concerning the real existence of the external world in order to ensure proper phenomenological procedure and consider 'the things themselves' as they are immediately presented to our conscious awareness. Thus for Husserl, the 'natural attitude' is simply our natural attachment to the external world that he thinks must be suspended so that one may directly grasp the structure of conscious awareness itself, as well as the objects of which one is conscious. Sartre uses Husserl's language to draw a parallel between our purifying reflection and the 'epoche', wherein our conscious awareness suspends its natural attachment to the world and disengages itself from the natural attitude without, however, contesting that it is still in the world, and must therefore act in the world among others. de Beauvoir is once again more helpful here than is Sartre, and the overlap of their respective views is striking:

> Existentialist conversion should rather be compared to Husserlian reduction: let man put his will to be "in parenthesis" and he will thereby be brought to the consciousness of his true condition. And just as the phenomenological reduction prevents the errors of dogmatism by suspending all affirmation concerning the mode of reality of the external world, whose flesh and bone presence the reduction does not, however, contest, so existentialist conversion does not suppress my instincts, desires, plans, and passions. It merely prevents any possibility of failure by refusing to set up as absolutes the ends toward which my transcendence thrusts itself, and by considering them in their connection with the freedom which projects them. (de Beauvoir 1991: 14)

Our 'natural' attachment to the world before conversion, for both

Sartre and de Beauvoir, constitutes the effort of our conscious activity to hide from itself behind an ego, which, they maintain, is never successful, since the very 'nature' of our existence is to be self-aware or self-conscious. That is, we are always pre-reflectively aware of our true condition as egoless, free, intentional beings whose entire reality is to be in relation to other persons and objects in the world. When, in impure reflection, we construct an ego that we view as determinative, we attempt to alter our relation between ourselves and the world, and pretend that we are no longer in danger before the world; we attempt to bar up the future rather than regard it as provisional. Hence impure reflection, preoccupied with the tainted goal of making the ego or self permanent and necessary, hides from us our spontaneous freedom, and reveals to us a self that is manufactured, rather than freely created.

In pure reflection, on the other hand, we recognize that values are freely created by us, rather than discovered or found. We do not view ourselves as merely the product of social, hereditary and environmental demands. In pure reflection we view ourselves as continuously active and intentional agents inscribing value into the world. Pure reflection discloses to us that we have no enduring or stable 'I' and that our very existence involves a process of becoming more than what we have been. In pure reflection I recognize my past as *there* (like a mermaid with her tail, Sartre says), but I recognize it as always open to new meaning and interpretation, not as something that has made me what I am now. In this sense we are not, in Sartre's view, free to 'wipe the slate clean' with respect to our past, but we are always free to give it new meaning – to *reinterpret* it. Similarly, I will regard my future in pure reflection as not unfolding mechanically before me, but as *being made* perpetually by me. Sartre's constant emphasis on reflection as a form of action should alert us that pure reflection could never be contemplative because it is a form of willing.

In *Notebooks* Sartre describes pure reflection as the means by which authentic existence is possible. We are 'prompted' or 'solicited', he notes, to convert to a new type of existence wherein our project is called into question and freedom is adopted as a primary value. He suggests that pure reflection is solicited in response to our perpetual effort to regain ourselves – to establish identity with ourselves. In pure reflection I now recognize that I am separated from anything that might define me: I am not this jealousy or anger because I am separated from it by my implicit self-awareness that I can always retreat from these. Pure reflection, then, inspires another kind of existence: 'Man is the being whose existence is in question in his being and since the being of man is action, this means that his choice of being is at the same time in question in his being' (Sartre 1992: 473). Here, we may recall Sartre's denial of the principle of identity with respect to his claim that we 'are the being whose existence is action'. Given Sartre's ontology, one cannot sensibly conceive of (human) action – as over against the redistribution of buildings by a tornado – in any other terms.

The modifications brought about by pure reflection are for Sartre (1) 'a new authentic way of being oneself for oneself, which transcends . . . bad faith'; (2) 'A thematic grasping of freedom, of gratuity, of unjustifiability'; and (3) 'A new relation of man to his project: he is both inside and outside' (Sartre 1992: 473). Here we see that conversion solicits in me a new awareness that I am both situated in the world among others and free; it prompts me to see that I have an outside, which is to say that I may be 'for others' rather than against them. Here we can see that the recuperative effort of pure reflection that occasions conversion affirms us as never self-identical, and therefore, as always troubled. In authenticity we are willing to maintain the unstable and troubled freedom that we are; rather than alienate ourselves from this condition by attempting to hide behind an ego or identify ourselves with a permanent and fixed self defined by roles, qualities, states, an 'essence', we face our true ontological condition squarely and honestly. This is why in *Notebooks* Sartre specifically refers to the meaning of our conversion to authenticity as the rejection of self-alienation. We can readily see, then, how conversion signifies a modification away from self-alienation and towards a new way of existing one's life. Conversion signifies that I have renounced my pre-reflective project of wanting to attain necessary existence and, along with it, the impure reflection that has willed to continue the bad faith project of the desire to be necessary or self-identical.

Sartre suggests and explores in *Notebooks* the insight he made in *TE* that we might be able to make the possibility of pure reflection the basis for some sort of ethics. The idea is that much human misery and discord is, according to him, the result of subject–object relations of conflict among persons since, as we noted, cooperation is not our original ontological condition and is not guaranteed in advance. These human conflicts arise, he thinks, from our desire to mask our freedom from ourselves; we use the other in order to believe in a substantial self – in order to realize the impossible project to be a necessary being. And he thinks that pure reflection may provide a basis for some sort of ethics to the extent that it facilitates an encounter with oneself as a responsible freedom, where freedom is taken as a primary value. He shows, further, how our adopting freedom as a value is revealed by the ways in which I authentically believe in and actually live my situated freedom in the world among others. That is, through pure reflection I authentically recognize that the existence of others in the world is equal to my own. In Sartre's view, once one has adopted and willed for oneself an authentic mode of existence, there simply can be no existential priority of oneself over others, or of others over oneself. Here, the authentic attitude would equally rule out both 'egoism' and 'altruism' as possible moral attitudes towards others. It is in this sense that de Beauvoir remarks that existentialism refuses 'to deny a priori that separate existents can, at the same time, be bound to each other, that their individual freedoms can forge laws valid for all' (de Beauvoir 1991: 18).

CHAPTER 6

BEING FOR AND AGAINST OTHERS

> ... in discovering my inner being I discover the other person at the
> same time, like a freedom placed in front of me. Hence, let us at once
> announce the discovery of a world which we shall call inter-
> subjectivity; this is the world in which man decides what he is and
> what others are.
>
> (Sartre 1998: 38)

In *Notebooks*, Sartre attempts to deepen the 'we-relation' that is
established by cooperation and generosity. One of the ways in which
we may create the conditions for cooperation, he thinks, is by 'unveiling' and disclosing our own freedom as situated and responsible
in a world where, as de Beauvoir puts it, 'the other is my concern'.

Oppression, Sartre says, is 'when my free subjectivity is given as
inessential, my freedom is an epiphenomenon, my initiative is sub-
ordinated and secondary, when my activity is directed by the Other
and takes the Other as its end' (Sartre 1992: 366). But following a
conversion to authenticity I recognize the Other as an absolute
freedom and choose to unveil her as freedom. If I make the Other
exist and recognize her contingency while perpetually surpassing it,
I 'enrich' the world and the Other. I 'give meaning to the Other's
existence' and bring in view her fragility and vulnerability: 'in
authenticity I choose to unveil the Other' in all her finitude (Sartre
1992: 366). But how, we may wonder, do I do this, exactly? We have
noted that it is by 'the look' that I first grasp the Other as 'another
freedom in general' (Sartre 1992: 366). And grasping the Other by
the look must always come first: 'But this disquieting, undifferenti-
ated, and intermittent freedom is not the freedom of *this* Other; it is
the intuition of another freedom in general' (Sartre 1992: 366). The

'structure of freedom' implies that freedom is always concrete; that is, it must always be understood as some particular undertaking that is aiming towards a goal: We do not, Sartre notes, 'grasp the freedom of others except through its goal' (Sartre 1992: 366). But, we may grasp the goal of others in different ways: 'If I simply transcend it on the way toward my own goal, it becomes a thing' (Sartre 1992: 366). If, however, 'I grasp the work of the other as an absolute demand requiring my approbation and my agreement, I grasp the man in the process of making it as freedom' (Sartre 1992: 366). I could, of course, also express disapproval and disagreement in grasping the other's work; this is something Sartre would also have to allow. But in authenticity, I grasp the Other as

> within-the-world: which is to say that all at once on the basis of an absolute goal (an absolute relation to subjectivity), I suddenly discover the total contingency, the absolute fragility, the finitude, and the mortality of the one who is proposing this goal to himself. With this I unveil the being-within-the-world of the one who through his freedom is surpassing the world and demanding that I surpass it. (Sartre 1992: 501)

To unconditionally accept the Other in all of her fragility and vulnerability is for Sartre to reveal her project and to love her authentically: 'Here we are able to understand what loving signifies in its authentic sense: I love if I create the contingent finitude of the Other as being-within-the-world in assuming my own subjective finitude and in willing this subjective finitude . . . Through me there is a vulnerability of the Other . . .' (Sartre 1992: 501). Here, Sartre is saying that to authentically reveal and unveil the Other is to take a genuine interest in, and to invest oneself in the Other's project. It is to grasp the project of the Other 'in terms of his relation to the world he is illuminating' (Sartre 1992: 502). Through revealing the Other's qualities I may see the kind of world she is illuminating: 'Through me, the Other's qualities appear, which can only exist for me and through my own upsurge. For example, the other becomes witty if I exist. He cannot be witty for himself. To be witty is to reveal a certain new, unexpected, humorous aspect of the world, filled with insight' (Sartre 1992: 507). If, Sartre, says, the Other is ignorant, I unveil his ignorance in a particular kind of way: 'So, beyond finitude and fragility, I unveil ignorance . . . But this ignorance not being lived in the first place, it comes to the man through me. Contingency, finitude, fragility, ignorance are all ways of being that I unveil in the existent as such' (Sartre 1992: 505). I may unveil the Other's ignorance so that it becomes for her a justification for failure and a reason for no longer trying. Or I may unveil the Other's ignorance so that my unveiling becomes for her an opportunity to ask for deeper challenges and to try to become more than she is now. In the former case, the Other is unveiled in bad faith because I treat her freedom as a thing by thwarting it and closing off possibilities for enrichment; the Other's ignorance becomes for her an absolute obstacle that is in the way, rather than a hindrance which may be surpassed. Sartre says that 'Ignorance is a mode of inter-human relations. Its type is that of refusal in the sense that to be judged ignorant by others acts as a cause does on my freedom' (Sartre 1992: 294). To disclose the Other's ignorance as a refusal is to render her inefficacious and incomplete; it is to do *violence* to her:

> In this way nothing about my freedom gets explained, instead the accent is put on what I am not, my internal finitude becomes an external limit and gets transformed into *incompleteness*. And since I possess my incomplete truth which appears as such to the eyes of the other as complete truth, I myself appear to these eyes of the other as incomplete ... Hence the other holds a part of me. He grasps himself as doing so and I, who grasp the other as knowing that he knows that I do not know, I grasp him as possessing that part of me that would allow me to be effective in the world and to be a present totality instead of being a past incompleteness. So through the existence of the other, the ignorance that was *nothing* or merely an abstract stop in the movement of knowing becomes a negative power that pierces me, reifies me, and makes me dependent on the other. (Sartre 1992: 299)

To the extent that this kind of 'unveiling by refusing' is exploited by the Other, the situation can become tragic. A child, for example, who hears from an angry teacher or parent 'You are lazy and stupid; you will never amount to anything' will experience their unveiling by the Other as a refusal that will be difficult to surpass because they may adopt it as true and definitive. But in the main, and where there is an absence of oppression, Sartre grants that the 'state' of experiencing incompleteness in the face of the Other's refusal

> can be considered *provisory* (for example, the child who will go to school) and as a condition to surpass so as to become an efficacious factor in the world. Freedom accepts being made part of the past and repetition so as to attain the moment when it will spring ahead into a new, fresh world that no one will steal from it. (Sartre 1992: 299)

However, things are quite different, he notes, when ignorance is disclosed by the Other such that the person who is ignorant experiences her ignorance as definitive and as not being reciprocal, 'as happens in an oppressive society' (Sartre 1992: 299). Sartre offers an example of 'reciprocal ignorance': 'I do not know medicine, but the medical doctor does not know philosophy. Each one holds the secret to the other's incompleteness. The one to whom I am an object is an object for me and in this way I deliver myself from my alienation' (Sartre 1992: 299). But an oppressed person, he says, who is

> reduced to servile labor or a wage earner who cannot get further education will live out his ignorance in the manner indicated. But further, to the extent that his ignorance is definitive, he will take up in anger or uneasiness that truth, which is necessarily incomplete and where the others, who constitute it definitively as incomplete and inefficacious, and who, by this very fact, shut him up in the only efficacy available to him: his servile labor. (Sartre 1992: 505)

Similarly, de Beauvoir reminds us of a statement made by George Bernard Shaw that an oppressive society relegates the shoeshine boy to the role of shining shoes and from this it is inferred that he is good for nothing other than shining shoes.

We should note here that *Notebooks* constitutes Sartre's aborted attempt to formulate an ethics only on the level of interpersonal relations; oppression still obviously exists socially and politically; but these do not, *by themselves*, preclude the possibility of authentic relations among persons. That said, it is certainly true that oppressive and alienating social conditions may very well make the kind of authentic interpersonal relations Sartre thought was possible far more difficult to attain. Indeed, this is why Sartre states in *Saint Genet: Actor and Martyr* that the abstract separation Good and Evil 'expresses . . . the alienation of man. The fact remains that, in the historical situation, this synthesis cannot be achieved. Thus an Ethic which does not explicitly profess that it is *impossible today* contributes to the bamboozling and alienation of men. The ethical problem arises from the fact that Ethics is for us inevitable and at the same time impossible' (Sartre 1963: 186). And even more explicitly, in *What is Literature?* he states:

> Such is the present paradox of ethics: If I am absorbed in treating a few chosen persons as absolute ends, for example, my wife, my son, my friends, the needy person I happen to come across, if I am bent upon fulfilling all my duties toward them, I shall spend my life doing so; I shall be led *to pass over in silence* the injustices of the age, the class struggle, colonialism, Anti-Semitism, etc., and finally to *take advantage of oppression in order to do good.* (Sartre 1988: 221–22)

Here Sartre is plainly struggling with the question concerning the possibility of ethics at a time when alienation and oppression are still present. On the one hand, because of the historical situation of oppression and alienation he is saying that he is unable to formulate his promised ethics. But on the other hand, he wants to show how ethical action is still possible in a world of injustice. So the ethical 'systems' proposed by moral philosophers in the tradition have been merely ideal, and dishonest, too, because they have not recognized the impossibility of an ideal system of ethics in an unjust world. The tension, or contradiction, between ideal ethical systems and oppressive societies explains why Sartre insists that 'in attaining myself through conversion, I have refused the abstract in order to will the concrete, that is, the maximum of being, I value it in that it makes (the Other's) project a concrete and particular existence, much richer than any merely abstract dogma' (Sartre 1992: 507). Hence he says that the 'project that the authentic man of action pursues is never "the good of humanity" but rather is such and such particular circumstances' (Sartre 1992: 507). As we have seen, the conversion to authenticity is described by Sartre as a kind of *moral* conversion; he speaks, for example, of conceiving of an absolute conversion to intersubjectivity and states that 'this conversion is ethical' (Sartre 1992: 507). But how, we should ask, does Sartre actually link morality and authenticity?

i. AUTHENTICITY AND THE MORALITY

Authentic conscious activity maintains the tension between the perpetual striving or quest to achieve necessary being on the one hand, and the necessity of making oneself in the midst of being on the other. Here, Sartre notes that we tend, in bad faith, towards one of these extremes. That is, we tend to become the necessary foundation of our existence and so think that we are caused and determined to be who we are, and therefore not free to make ourselves, or we tend to lose ourselves in our 'transcendence', never completing projects or meeting goals. Authentic conscious activity does not attempt to collapse into pure being in a flight from its own anguish, and it does not lose itself in its own transcendence, such that the goal it proposes to itself is never reached. Conversion to authenticity is our willed resolve to accept ourselves as at risk before the world, and in doing so, it accepts and values itself as the gratuitous freedom it is. We can appreciate once again de Beauvoir's contribution and clarity on this point in *Ethics of Ambiguity*:

> To convert the absence into presence, to convert my flight into will, I must assume my project positively. It is not a matter of retiring into the completely inner and, moreover, abstract movement of a given spontaneity, but of adhering to the concrete and particular movement by which this spontaneity defines itself by thrusting itself toward an end. It is through this end that it sets up that my spontaneity confirms itself by reflecting upon itself. (de Beauvoir 1991: 26)

Authentic conscious activity, then, repudiates those frozen values that are created in what Sartre calls 'the spirit of seriousness that spring up as a result of its own bad faith project' (Sartre 1992: 480, 506). 'Spirit of seriousness' often has a pejorative meaning similar to the self-righteous earnestness of people who take themselves (and their role in society) too seriously. It resolves to 'take itself as its end' (Sartre 1991: 560) and to value itself as the freedom it is. This is the sense in which Sartre spoke in *BN* of our conscious activity's transformation as the transformation to the 'ethical plane' (Sartre 1956: 628).

We have seen that for Sartre the role of purifying reflection, as the means by which conversion to authenticity takes place, has a moral dimension. This moral dimension suggests that Sartre was concerned to show how one may change one's own personal values from a rejection of freedom to an acceptance of it. Insofar as conscious activity's rejection of freedom constitutes for him an alienation of the self from what it is, and thus constitutes a certain violence done, the transformation from that project will involve affirming oneself as autonomous: 'What therefore can the project of a reflection that refuses to look for Being be? It can only be a question of a radical decision for autonomy' (Sartre 1991: 478). By 'autonomous' Sartre certainly does not mean 'self-enclosed'; this interpretation would, of course, distort his entire project because, as we have seen, it is precisely insofar as we creatively undertake projects in the world that Sartre thinks we may create a world that will influence the lives of others – for better or worse. Once one has accepted adopted freedom as a value, and recognized that one is ultimately unjustifiable, Sartre thinks one will be able, in turn, to alter the way in which one values not only oneself, but others and the world as well: 'The For-itself is led to unveil for others, with others, in the service of others' (Sartre 1991: 485).

It should now be clear that Sartre wishes to connect authenticity with an ethical attitude. He speaks, for example, of an 'ethical reflection' that takes on the *moral being* of what is reflected upon as important (Sartre 1991: 5). He tells us that it is not a question of 'being good in the eyes of God or society', but rather 'It is a question of willing the Good (in the unreflected upon) in order to be ethical' (Sartre 1991: 5). And, finally, he notes, 'The one and only base of the moral life must be spontaneity that is, the immediate, the unreflective' (Sartre 1991: 5). Importantly, Sartre does not mean 'basis' as in 'biological facts are the basis of evolutionary theory', since, as we have seen, there is no notion of justification in his views.

By 'ethical reflection' Sartre clearly means 'pure' reflection that, as we know, refers to the momentary grasping of ourselves while not ceasing our activity. For example, as a teacher I engage in pure reflection when I momentarily become aware of myself as a teacher: what does it *mean* to be a teacher – what does it mean to be a member of the teaching profession in the twenty-first century? Or, if one works as a bond trader on Wall Street, one will ask oneself what it means to be a trader in the twenty-first century; the first thing one may notice is that, as a trader, one is upholding the economic system of capitalism, with all of the values it entails. Of equal importance, I become aware of the significance of my role as 'teacher' while not ceasing my activity of teaching, and while not turning my teaching into an object of reflection. What always remains absolutely crucial for Sartre is the intentional activity itself. The idea is that we do not contemplatively reflect upon our doing something, but that we do it; what is important is that our intention always be fulfilled in an act. In authenticity, then, we do not distract ourselves from these momentary 'flashes' of pure reflection or reflective self-awareness. In authenticity we allow our 'egos' to become momentarily 'awakened' so that the meaning of our activity is revealed. Sartre maintains that most persons live their lives uncritically because they don't question the meaning and purpose of their lives. Since our existence necessarily involves a being in the world among others, pure reflection is for Sartre 'ethical' to the extent that it solicits or prompts our having an outside – it reveals to us the significance of our having a self that is *for others*.

We want to be careful to note that when Sartre says that the 'base of the moral life' must be 'spontaneity', 'immediate' and 'unreflective', he is not talking about an ethics of sheer impulse or drive:

> And when it is said of existentialism, "so man is then free to choose by caprice," this is silly for many reasons, but especially because one is presupposing that choices are instantaneous and constantly renewed. The word "caprice" says it all: a man who is chance for himself. Whereas we are all destiny for ourselves. Not only can we not forge an ethics at the level of caprice – by replacing it with the instantaneous virtuous act – but even caprice itself, if it exists, is the sign of a whole condition and a whole project surpassing this condition. (Sartre 1992: 47)

Sartre's claim, then, is that it is only through action, or through the way in which we *exist* in the world, that the world might be changed. The important question for him is not what we are, but who we are now, and how we live our freedom; some of the most important moral questions concerning our existence can only be worked out by existing. We have said that Sartre understood pure reflection as the *means by which* conversion to authenticity is achieved, and as an intention that has a moral dimension. Although he conceives of conversion as moral, he insists 'In the absence of . . . historical change, there is no absolute conversion . . . Just as the rejection of war does not suppress war, whatever else it may accomplish' (Sartre 1991: 9). Here, as we have noted, because there exists historical oppression, absolute moral conversion is not possible today; but individual conversion that would have implications for the moral life on the local or social level, he thinks, is still possible.

Freedom implies for Sartre ontological and existential responsibility: How do we live our freedom? How do we create ourselves in a world that resists us? How do we confirm others in their freedom? Because conversion to authenticity involves the rejection of transcendent values and an acceptance of oneself as the contingent source of values, Sartre claims that to be authentic is to also be responsible:

> For the authentic man's greatness . . . derives necessarily from his misery or contingency. Because he is a point of view, finitude, contingency, ignorance, he makes there be a world, that is, he can take on all at once the responsibility for himself and for the universe. And the universal itself or essence . . . can appear only by starting from the limitation of some point of view. The universal or the possibility of perpetually surpassing my finitude. (Sartre 1992: 493, 509)

In authenticity I affirm and value my concrete freedom, which implies at the same time that I affirm and value the concrete freedom of human reality in general. That is, because we live in what de Beauvoir and Sartre refer to as a 'peopled world', in authenticity we extend ourselves in such a way that we reach the other's project or, as Sartre says, we 'unveil' them in all their vulnerability and finitude. To adopt the other's project as part of my own, and to help her to express her freedom is to affirm human reality insofar as she is a part of human reality. In this respect, one adopts a way of being that is consistent with and faithful to the human condition in its fragility, ignorance and uncertainty. Of course, one may also choose inauthentically; the inauthentic choice is a choice that Sartre does – and must – allow for, given his claim that we are ontologically free.

In *Notebooks* Sartre repeatedly suggests that insofar as I treat the Other as less than free or, in the language of Kant, as merely a means to my own end, I do violence to her and to myself. He regards this inauthentic choice as dishonest and in bad faith. In his speech 'The Humanism of Existentialism', he claims that we can judge others to be inauthentic on the basis of truth and falsity, where dishonesty is a kind of falsehood. Since one always makes a choice in relationship to others, a certain kind of judgement is possible:

> First, one can judge (and this is perhaps not a judgment of value, but a logical judgment) that certain choices are based on error and others on truth. If we have defined man's situation as a free choice, with no excuses and no recourse, every man who takes refuge behind the excuse of his passions, every man who sets up a determinism, is a dishonest man. (Sartre 1990: 44–5)

de Beauvoir reinforces the notion of the 'dishonest attitude' in *The Ethics of Ambiguity*:

> However, even among proponents of secular ethics, there are many who charge existentialism with offering no objective content to the moral act. It is said that this philosophy is subjective, even solipsistic. If he is once enclosed within himself, how can man get out? But there too we have a great deal of dishonesty. It is rather well known that the fact of being a subject is a universal fact . . . By affirming that the source of all values resides in the freedom of man, existentialism merely carries on the tradition of Kant, Fichte, and Hegel . . . The idea that defines all humanism is that the world is not a given world, foreign to man, one to which he has to force himself to yield from without. It is the world willed by man, insofar as his will expresses his genuine reality. (de Beauvoir 1991: 16–17)

Sartre goes on to wonder what if someone were to ask, 'But what if I choose to be dishonest?' and replies, 'There's no reason for you not to be, but I'm saying that that's what you are, and the strictly coherent attitude is that of honesty . . . Dishonesty is obviously a falsehood because it belies the complete freedom of involvement' (Sartre 1990: 45). Moreover, he says that it is even possible to make a kind of *moral* judgement with respect to one's dishonesty:

... I can bring moral judgment to bear. When I declare that freedom in every concrete circumstance can have no other aim than to want itself, if man has once become aware that in his forlornness he imposes values he can no longer want but one thing, and that is freedom as the basis of all values. That doesn't mean he wants it in the abstract. It means simply that the ultimate meaning of the acts of honest men is the quest of freedom as such ... we want freedom for freedom's sake and in every particular circumstance. (Sartre 1990: 45–6).

But what *kind* of moral judgement can Sartre advance against one who is being dishonest or incoherent? Surely, on his account one may choose to be dishonest or incoherent; human beings have no absolute obligation to be reasonable or logically consistent, since these have no objective value. Perhaps Sartre's point is that to want freedom as the basis of all my values is to want freedom to be *willed* by me as my primary and highest value. It might be argued that Sartre refers to the 'coherent' attitude as a 'logical' or 'conceptual' standard or requirement, notwithstanding that he would also have to allow that one may freely choose to value irrationality and inconsistency; again, neither these nor their opposites have any objective validity. Is Sartre presupposing that logical consistency and a coherent attitude have intrinsic objective value? Is he allowing something like the Kantian 'principle of universalizability', the view that I may not will a maxim or act unless I am able to, at the same time, will that it become a universal law for everyone, to slip in? But Sartre maintains that the choice to be rational is *itself* 'beyond all reasons' and 'prior to all logic' (Sartre 1956: 479, 570), so he cannot be saying that reason and logic have any value in themselves, other than the value that persons confer on them. When Sartre says that the 'strictly coherent attitude' requires that freedom be chosen as my primary value because it is the absolute source of all meaning and value, he must mean something other than 'coherent' in the logical or epistemic sense.

Philosophers on both sides of the Atlantic have attempted to defend Sartre by interpreting his views on morality as Kantian. While it is certainly true that Sartre was deeply influenced by Kant, and especially preoccupied with him in *Notebooks*, it would be a mistake to suppose that his views parallel those of Kant. The perceptive adage that one may be best known not only by the friends one keeps, but by the enemies they never cease fighting, fits well here. Sartre's marked hostility to Kant's ideas manifests something more than mere opposition to his thought; it tells us something significant about Sartre's own views, as well as those to which he was decidedly (one might also say, *viscerally*) opposed.

CHAPTER 7

THE WEIGHT OF IMMANUEL KANT

Freedom is existence, and in it existence precedes essence. The upsurge of freedom is immediate and concrete and is not to be distinguished from its choice; that is, from the person himself.

(Sartre 1998: 66)

As we noted in the previous chapter, the perceptive adage that one can best know a philosopher by the enemies he never stops fighting is particularly relevant to Sartre's relationship to the great German philosopher Immanuel Kant. Throughout his writings Sartre, and especially in *Notebooks*, one can see a marked hostility to the moral philosophy of Kant. Sartre's steadfast opposition, for example, to the central Kantian claim that moral conduct consists in obeying abstractly knowable maxims, valid independently of situation, that is, independent of historical, social and political time and place, is particularly noteworthy:

To whom is the ethical demand addressed? To the abstract universal? But then it loses all its meaning and becomes abstract and formal itself, since the concrete—that is, social—situation may change. If one says, "Act in such a way, other things being equal," this demand loses all its meaning since it refers to the eternal return. The problem of collaboration or resistance: there is a concrete moral choice. Kantianism teaches nothing on this subject. (Sartre 1992: 7)[1]

Such opposition may at first seem puzzling since Sartre has been widely interpreted as invoking at least *some* elements of Kant's moral philosophy. To be sure, this interpretation is reinforced by the fact that Sartre most certainly did borrow key ideas and even exact phrasing from Kant, which he then radically modified for his own purposes. But it would be a mistake to interpret Sartre's views on morality as 'Kantian' or as even marginally endorsing Kant's views. It seems far more plausible to view Sartre's continuing preoccupation (one might even say, 'obsession') with Kant as indicating a path he did *not* wish to take with respect to the most promising moral terrain (*le terrain moral*). Starting with Sartre is thus to start with his nemesis, Kant, especially regarding the question of how we are to live morally.

In another provocative passage from *Notebooks* that suggests a disapproval of Kant's approach, Sartre declares that '... even though the possible, and therefore the universal, is a necessary structure of action, we must return to the individual drama of the finite series "Man" when the deepest ends of existence are at issue. To the finite and historical source of possibilities. To this society. Ethics is an individual, subjective and historical enterprise' (Sartre 1992: 7). What Sartre seems to be suggesting here is that any moral theory that ignores or denies the peculiar ontological status or condition of persons would stand self-condemned, unless morality is not strictly a *human affair*. We have seen that Sartre's phenomenological investigation in *BN* has shown that we exist freely in concrete situations with others, and that my conscious awareness is not in the first instance reflectively rational or conceptual, but it is pre-reflectively engaged as an intentional awareness that directs itself not inwards, but outwards into a world of possibility.

While offering a sustained review of Kant's moral philosophy would take us beyond the scope of our investigation, we will consider the most salient of Kant's views on morality that will serve as necessary background. Then, we will offer a more detailed account of Kant's views, over against Sartre's, and try to elucidate and crystallize some of Sartre's criticisms of Kant's moral philosophy, particularly in *Notebooks*. In the final section, we will explore a longstanding and continuing debate among Sartre commentators as to whether or not Sartre may plausibly be understood to accept the Kantian principle of universability, briefly noted in the previous chapter. This view has been recognized on all sides as crucial to one's assessment of Sartre's view.

i. KANT'S VIEW OVER AGAINST SARTRE'S:
PRELIMINARY OBSERVATIONS

The very first thing to notice is that for Kant moral principles are grounded in reason and so commanded categorically. Because they are grounded in reason alone, they are understood to be objectively valid and necessary. According to Kant, the nature of morality is such that its principles are legitimate by reason alone, and the moral worth of a person is determined only insofar as she has acted not merely in accordance with duty, but out of duty and respect for the moral law. To violate the moral law or to fail to give the moral law to oneself would be a violation of reason itself; it would constitute a failure to be rational. Only reason, Kant insists, could produce in us a good will, a will that is good without qualification: '. . . since none the less reason has been imparted to us as a practical power – that is, one which is to have influence on the will; its true function must be to produce a will which is good, not as a means to further some end, but in itself' (Kant 1964: 61–4). Kant also insists that we are the lawgiver – that through reason we are able to give the moral law to ourselves: 'A man who propounds that a law which in accordance with his will shall be binding on others, promulgates a law, and is a lawgiver' (Kant 1964: 17/50–1).

Given Sartre's phenomenological ontology, there are several ways in which he finds Kant's views troubling. Before offering Sartre's critique, however, we first need to examine a critical statement offered by de Beauvoir against Kant that elucidates the broader disagreement. Although Kantian ethics, she notes, 'is at the origin of all ethics of autonomy, it is very difficult for Kant to account for an evil will' (de Beauvoir 1991: 33). In Kant's view, de Beauvoir says, the evil will becomes a non-rational will:

> As the choice of his character the subject makes is achieved in the intelligible world by a purely rational will, one cannot understand how the latter expressly rejects the law which it gives to itself. But this is because Kantianism defined man as a pure positivity, and it therefore recognized no other possibility in him than coincidence with himself . . . Only unlike Kant, we do not see man as being essentially a positive will. On the contrary, he is first defined as negativity. He is first at a distance from himself. He can coincide with himself only by agreeing never to rejoin

himself . . . And it is precisely because an evil will is here possible that the words "to will oneself free" have a meaning. (de Beauvoir 1991: 33)

Indeed, as Dostoevski's Underground Man shows us, it is always possible to choose the non-ethical and still be perfectly rational. For Sartre too, an evil will and a rational will are not incompatible: 'Man is the source of good and evil and judges himself in the name of the good and evil he creates. Therefore, a priori neither good nor evil' (Sartre 1992: 17). And in his 'speech', *Existentialism*, Sartre remarks, 'Nowhere is it written that Good exists, that we must not lie; because the fact is we are on a plane where there are only men' (Sartre, Jean-Paul, *Existentialism and Human Emotions*. Carol Publishing, New Jersey, 1998: 22). Contrary to Kant, both Sartre and de Beauvoir insist upon freedom from the moral authority of any putative God, Reason or any other absolute standard by which we might judge our actions. Both philosophers argue that one is always free to reject whatever standard is presented; this is why in their view freedom truly is *itself* a value. If the rationality of one's moral principles of action is argued to be the ultimate authoritative normative justification, one is always free to reject reason. If God is posited as the ultimate source of value, one is always free to adopt atheism or to be irreverent.

To be sure, on Kant's view, too, one is not compelled to will according to the categorical imperative. Indeed, he allows that we can and do violate the categorical imperative all the time, but on his view we do not do so 'freely'. Here, the difference between Sartre and Kant could not be starker: one may simply freely refuse, on Sartre's account, to give 'the law' to oneself; it is in anguish, Sartre says, that I realize that I am not the lawgiver, but the lawmaker.[2] Indeed, in giving 'the law' to oneself, Sartre argues that one may very well limit and circumscribe one's possibilities: 'But if *judgment* (in the Kantian sense) retains a place . . . then the regulative and normative end intervenes as an imperative. That is, one can stop seeing its concrete tie to the situation in order to grasp it only as an interdiction, a restriction or an internal refusal' (Sartre 1992: 162). Here, Sartre is noting the particular, situated, individual and subjective character of morality over against Kant's emphasis on the objective, pure, necessary and absolute.

As we have seen, the will for Kant is said to be 'good without qualification' insofar as it makes correct rational choices in accordance with what reason demands. Speaking about 'the will' in this way was foreign to Sartre, involving a false psychology – as his phenomenological ontology of the sort of being peculiar to humans had already claimed to show – in which freedom falsely becomes understood as a property of something. For Sartre, a 'good will', insofar as he would accept the term, 'will' is not one that makes correct rational choices, but a for-itself being that sees itself as always making choices. Conversely, a 'bad will' would not be a for-itself being that chooses irrationally, but one that does not see itself as choosing freely.

ii. DUTY, DEMAND AND OBLIGATION

In *The War Diaries* Sartre tells us that the morality of duty never interested him: '. . . however much I was told that the categorical imperative expressed the autonomy of my will, I didn't believe a word of it. I have always wanted my freedom to be above morality, not below it' (Sartre, Jean-Paul, *The War Diaries: November 1939/ March 1940*, trans. Quintin Hoare, New York: Pantheon Books, 1984: 34). And in another passage Sartre declares with what is probably an exasperated tone, '. . . morality based on duty: all that's hidden beneath that shameful formula, with its Kantian ring: I have only the right to do my duty . . . In the end, I can't really see anything but a moral code based on authenticity escaping the reproach of complacency' (Sartre 1984: 94). And, again, in *Notebooks* Sartre is no less dismissive of an 'ethics of duty': 'This alienated freedom that makes itself impersonal in itself, negating everything about itself in order to realize an abstract and unconditioned will that is revealed to it by others who are its impersonal *bearers*, is duty, that absolute obligation each one of us can demand from the others . . .' (Sartre 1992: 267). And again: 'This is exactly what it is for Kant. I treat the freedom *in the other* as an end, even over against him. This means that I refuse to recognize his freedom as him' (Sartre 1992: 269).[3] Since the ethics of duty involves for Sartre an inescapably alienated freedom, it is, he says, 'the passage to the metaphysical state of theological ethics' (Sartre 1992: 268) and 'the sacrifice of man to the *human*' (Sartre 1992: 272), where it remains abstract, not concrete and situated. Sartre does not believe that the categorical imperative or the ethics of duty, as understood by Kant, genuinely expresses the autonomy of the will because human freedom for Kant is circumscribed by obligation, and thus becomes a choice of a self that is defined in advance by another rather than a choice of a world that reflects and expresses the particular inscription of a self in the world: 'The freedom that for Kant upholds the categorical imperative is noumenal, therefore the freedom of *another*' (Sartre 1992: 139).

Throughout *Notebooks* Sartre is critical of the idea of 'demand' in ethics insofar as it is understood as an unconditioned imperative or obligation in Kant's sense. He states, for example, 'a demand conceals the ruse whereby I can be free only by realizing (making real, carrying out) this demand' (Sartre 1992: 257).[4] Demands and obligations are for him not only mechanisms of deception, but they are ultimately alienating and oppressive:

> Deception is the result for people to whom one says: 'you only did your duty,' that is, those who want to recognize themselves in the result of their operation (generosity); but one shows them that there was just a realization of their duty. The person who acts out of duty does not recognize himself in his work. Acting by himself, inventing his own means, this person wants to find his free activity in so doing, but since he is alienated by another choice, he perpetually recognizes someone other than himself. (Sartre 1992: 256)

Sartre notes that the ambiguity of Kant's position is that (1) 'I do my duty in order to be pure freedom and it is in pure freedom that I accede to ethics' absolute, through the affirmation that the human realm is unconditional – the proposed end lies *in its materiality*, which is creative of value', and (2) 'I participate in this value as a necessary instrument for realizing it' (Sartre 1992: 257). This 'mystification', he notes, has the advantage of keeping my freedom 'safe from anxiety' and of perpetuating an attitude of resignation. Duty, Sartre says, '. . . is discharged of any anxiety by that freedom in back of freedom that takes it upon itself to decide upon my ends.[5] My freedom is no longer constituting and creative, but rather realizing. It no longer has its task to bring about the world of ethics, but just to maintain it'.[6] This ambiguity reveals the 'thinglikeness of such freedom' because 'sometimes freedom is given for me as the *a priori* structure of my projects and sometimes I feel myself *as given* for freedom inasmuch as it is another's constituting freedom' (Sartre 1992: 257). Sartre notes that in Kant's theory of rational moral choice 'the *percipi* of obligation is distinct from its *esse* . . . It is just this aspect of coming up on me from behind that Kant expressed . . .' (Sartre 1992: 253). But since the obligation remains outside of me, it is indifferent to me; I remain inessential in the face of Kant's conception:

> But obligation lies behind this temporality and renders it inessential. My temporality, like all my structures, is rendered inessential by the presence-in-the-rear of obligation. This is, in effect, an immediate and a-temporal (eternal) relation of the project and its end. Therefore it runs through all my projects and surpasses them as inessential and subordinate projects. Behind me, I have the presence of this demand, and in front of me, on the horizon of my projects, the end as connected to this obligation. (Sartre 1992: 253)

For Sartre, then, such obligation 'does not appear head on but from the rear . . . Because it is, in fact, not the end to be realized (which always stands over against me) but a claim on my decision to realize this end . . . (It) is a back door kind of transcendence, that is, it lies behind the very source of my freedom . . . However, it gets distinguished from this freedom because, as obligation, it is in the dimension of being' (Sartre 1992: 253). Freedom that is 'born from the foundation' of a demand, an obligation or a duty, however, is not gratuitous freedom, and therefore, does not need to invent its goals. But for Sartre, the very meaning of freedom is to invent goals, and to be able, therefore, to conceive of a different kind of world. Although Sartre agrees with Kant that what is fundamental to morality is the responsible and freely chosen act, he claims that there is little point in speaking of free and responsible choice if the values that are 'chosen' are given antecedently in terms of duties, obligations and demands.

iii. DOES SARTRE ACCEPT KANT'S UNIVERSABILITY PRINCIPLE?

In light of Sartre's objections to Kant's moral theory in *Notebooks*, it seems especially propitious to weigh in once again on the question of whether Sartre may reasonably be interpreted as invoking or endorsing Kant's principle of universability (*Allgemeinheit*) in a strictly formal, vacuous version.

The question concerning whether or not Sartre accepts the Kantian principle of universability has received much attention over the years. The idea of universability in ethics is most commonly associated with the moral philosophy of Kant, and has been defended by contemporary moral theorists, most notably, R. M. Hare, in *Freedom and Reason* and 'Universalisability' in *Proceedings of the Aristotelian Society*. Although distinct meanings of the term 'universalization' may be distinguished, we are concerned with the meaning given by Kant in his formulation of the categorical imperative:

> Since I have robbed the will of every inducement that might arise for it as a consequence of obeying any particular law, nothing is left but the conformity of actions to universal law as such, and this alone must serve the will as its principle. That is to say, I ought never to act except in such a way that I can also will that my maxim should become a universal law. (Kant 1964: 69–70)

Some commentators have claimed that Sartre contradictorily 'sold out' to the principle of universalizability, and so undermined the phenomenological ontology he presented in *Being and Nothingness*.[7] Other philosophers, most notably, Alisdair MacIntyre and Gilbert Harman, have argued that Sartre denies the principle of universalizability and advocates only a 'personal consistency' requirement with respect to one's moral principles.[8] Still others, perhaps more generously, interpret Sartre as accepting the principle of universalizability without inconsistency.[9] These philosophers generally argue that Sartre's commitment to the Kantian principle allows him to ground and justify the moral choices that are so central to his ethics. The principle of universalizability, they claim, is necessary in order for Sartre to be able to distinguish particular acts of choice from choices that are merely arbitrary or capricious. Notably, Sartre himself has addressed this view by pointing out that it does not necessarily follow that choice is arbitrary merely because one does not invoke an *a priori* principle such as the Kantian principle. He notes that we are all obliged 'to choose an attitude, and if I in any way assume responsibility for a choice which, *in involving myself, also involves all mankind* this has nothing to do with caprice, even if no *a priori* value determines my choice' (Sartre 1998: 41).[10] To be sure, Sartre's statement does not itself constitute an argument but, as I hope to show, he does offer defensible reasons as to why he thinks he can avoid the charge of caprice or chance.

In addition to those who think that Sartre either 'sold out to', rejected or accepted the principle of universalizability, there are those who cannot decide exactly what Sartre's view is.[11]

More recently, David Pellauer, translator of Sartre's *Notebooks*, has remarked, 'Somehow, "man" . . . slides from the particular existing individual I am to humanity in general. . . . Critics have seen this as a kind of unacknowledged Kantian element in Sartre's remarks on ethics that is difficult to account for especially on the basis of *Being and Nothingness*' (Sartre 1992: xii). And in an article on Sartre's popular 'speech' on Existentialism, the principal source wherein it is alleged that Sartre endorses universalizability, Terry Keefe notes that while universalizability plays a role in Sartre's ethics, the status or nature of that role has been questioned. What has seemed so controversial, he says, is

> Whether universalizability in ethics is a concept that arises as a logical consequence out of metaphysical or ontological foundations of Sartre's existentialism. It has been implied that, on the contrary, universalizability is to be seen as a kind of expedient in the text of "L'Existentialism," as an unfounded, almost arbitrary attempt to avoid some of the obviously unpalatable moral consequences of Sartre's emphasis on the individual's freedom and moreover, an expedient which is inconsistent with the views expressed in *Being and Nothingness*. (Keefe 1988: 84–5)

The debate over the role of universalizability in Sartre's thought suggests, I think, a misunderstanding of his views on moral agency. The participants in the discussion are mistaken in that they are committed to accepting certain assumptions concerning moral agency that Sartre himself did not accept. These assumptions cannot be made if we take seriously Sartre's early theory of human consciousness, presented in *The Transcendence of the Ego*, as well as the moral implications of his phenomenological ontology, presented in *Notebooks*. The assumptions that may be called into question are (1) that Sartre is referring to universal principles or maxims, and (2) that Sartre allows for a noumenal subject, one that might therefore be capable of discovering universalizing moral principles. It seems, then, that Sartre is wrongly supposed to be dragging in the Kantian principle – whether consistently or inconsistently.[12] Sartre's claim that the ego is 'transcendent' – not, be it noted, transcendental – is not only conceptually adequate, but it is able to explain and defend his stronger claim that when we choose, we are choosing for *all* of humanity.

To be sure, there are passages from Sartre's works that strongly suggest that he endorses Kant's principle. But when Sartre states that in each of our acts we are responsible not just for ourselves, but for all persons, he is stating, a usual interpretation notwithstanding, something quite different from what Kant is stating in the categorical imperative.

iv. THE FIRST MISTAKEN ASSUMPTION

The first mistaken assumption that the debate rests on is that in the various passages that are often cited, Sartre is claiming that moral and immoral conduct involves universal principles, rules or maxims. If Sartre were talking about universal 'principles' or 'maxims' one could rightly claim that he is invoking universality.

It is crucial to notice a distinction between universality and both the ultimate particularity of our chosen actions, and the generality they nonetheless involve. While Sartre rejects Kant's claim that there can be universal maxims for moral choice, he does not claim, as some critics have charged, that we do not *generalize* our moral and nonmoral choices. Indeed, if it were true that Sartre placed exclusive emphasis on the ultimate particularity of our moral choices, then critics would be right to object that the moral choice for him cannot be distinguished from sheer caprice or chance. But of course Sartre would agree that we generalize when we deliberate; the important point for him, however, is that I recognize that *my generalization is always mine*. My generalization of a particular (rather than universal) principle, then, is not attributable to 'science' or 'religion' or 'society', but to this action here and now. For Sartre, then, every particular action 'A' is a *sort* of action of mine. These dimensions are inseparable. The general principle constitutes my moral justification, but it has no universal standing; and like all moral generalizations, it is clearly optional, one possibility among others.

Sartre certainly grants that there is no question that we reflect and invent in terms of generalities. However, these are (a) not universalizations, and (b) not authorized by anyone or anything (God, a noumenal self, or Reason as such), except by my free decision to act on my chosen maxim. Sartrean moral and immoral conduct, then, refers to our ability to generalize particular actions in the world (e.g. to join the Resistance or to remain with one's mother),[13] while always 'owning' that generalization as *mine*. Indeed, one of the most important ways in which Sartre is different from Kant is that he rejects the claim that principles of correct action can be justified independently of their proposed application to any particular action in the world. For Sartre, a 'principle' exists only insofar as it is applied to decisions to act.

Sartre denies, then, the *a priori* relevance of any principle, whether universal or general, and he denies that there are universal principles that could support one choice over against another. He maintains that persons choose their principles as they make their decisions, and these decisions are generally made from within one's fundamental project or original choice of oneself. Once one decides, one has freely legislated an action in a particular situation, notwithstanding that one also locates the act in a context of general considerations (instances of family loyalty vs. instances of party solidarity, for example). Now this manifestly does not mean, as some critics have charged, that Sartre is forging an ethics on the level of caprice. With respect to the problem of caprice, Sartre commentator Joseph Catalano has noted that it is not true that Sartre is an irrationalist just because he maintains that actions are what are primarily intelligible. Importantly, Catalano observes, although 'reason has an ambiguous relation to freedom ... this ambiguity does not have to be uncritical' (Catalano 1996: 5/84). Indeed, we have already appreciated that the authentic attitude will freely adopt a critical stance by embracing freedom as a primary value.

On Sartre's account persons forge, both individually and collectively, principles, maxims and rules of conduct; these can only be moral generalizations which concern the human world (not 'in-themselves' beings) and hence, have no universal standing, much less objective standing. And we are responsible insofar as we choose to sustain these or move beyond them.

Kant, Sartre says, 'believes that the formal and the universal are enough to constitute an ethics. We, on the other hand, think that principles which are too abstract run aground in trying to decide action' (Sartre 1998: 47). In the well known example concerning whether the young man ought to remain with his mother or join the Free French forces, it is the *particular action* in that time and place, Sartre says, not some general maxim or rule of conduct, that the young man is responsible for. So the whole notion of universality has no grip: I may very well choose to *universalize a general maxim or principle*, for example, 'Family before Country' or 'Country before Family'. But I cannot universalize an *actual deed* in the world. In this respect, Sartre notes,

> The universal is a category of being-part-of-the-world, not of being-in-the-world. The qualities that constitute the universal essence are *given*, they are static, part of an eternity concerning which one may just as well say that it is a past eternal (*Wesen ist was gewesen ist*). Man, who through his negativity breaks every form that encloses him, continually pushes outward the limits of what man is. (Sartre 1992: 69)

For Sartre 'Ethics is an individual, subjective, and historical enter-prise' because 'the possible man comes from the concrete one . . . We are such that the possible becomes possible starting from us' (Sartre 1992: 5–6).

We have seen that throughout *Notebooks* Sartre is critical of the Kantian universal and states that correctly understood, ethics must be concrete; which *does not*, the reader should note, *exclude* general-ities as chosen. He states, for example, that no Kantian universal principle is available to tell us what we ought to do in a particular situation, because the particular, the concrete exists, but the uni-versal does not. With respect to the question of collaboration or resistance, for instance, Sartre states, 'there is a concrete moral choice. Kantianism teaches nothing on this subject' (Sartre 1992: 7). The Kantian imperative 'Do Not Lie', he says, means '. . . in no case no matter the situation. In other words the world is inessential. Let us also add: my life, my projects, my desires' (Sartre 1992: 254). Here Sartre is emphasizing that situations can only be ascertained via reflection, hence via concepts, hence via generalities. But such generalities are never imposed on us. The Kantian prescription 'Tell the Truth', he says, 'leaps over the situation where there might be a possibility of telling a lie. And since it does not participate in my situation, it gives itself as a freedom beyond any situation, or as pure freedom ... it is freedom frozen into eternity in the very instant that it chooses' (Sartre 1992: 254). The demand or duty not to lie, says Sartre, 'implies a confidence in the human order and an indifference to the world (such that) the world can never be conceived of as an absolute resistance' (Sartre 1992: 238). Sartre is here insisting again on the *givenness of the situation* in which we are acting or refusing to act – versus Kant. It seems clear, then, that Sartre is not referring to Kantian universal maxims or principles since Kant has found experience itself to be an unsatisfactory grounding for morality: 'In actual fact it is absolutely impossible for experience to establish with complete certainty a single case in which the maxim of an action in other respects right has rested solely on moral grounds and on the thought of one's duty ... for when moral value is in question, we are concerned not with the actions which we see, but with their inner principles, which we cannot see' (Kant 1964: 74–5).

v. THE SECOND MISTAKEN ASSUMPTION

Sartre claims that all persons have a pre-reflective awareness of themselves as free – as being able to call both the world itself, and their place in the world, into question. But because we have seen that Sartre maintains that our awareness of ourselves as the free source of value in the world is daunting, we very often seek to hide in bad faith our awareness of our freedom. It is only in moments of what Sartre calls 'pure reflection' that we may catch a glimpse of ourselves as wholly free, and thereby as the unique source of value in the world, that we may be said to adopt an attitude of authenticity. But authenticity is not itself a static state of consciousness; it is fleeting and must be sustained by our re-affirmation of ourselves and our world as a value to be pursued, rather than as a self or world that is. Sartre's conception of the self as a value to be pursued rather than something that is and his rejection of the existence of an 'I' or 'inner' self that inhabits consciousness constitute the second reason why he cannot be said to accept Kant's universability principle.

Although Kant recognizes that we cannot meaningfully speak of responsibility, obligation, duty or morality, unless we presuppose freedom, he is unable to prove that we are in fact free. Kant offers a 'two-standpoints' view of persons that allows him to reconcile the antinomy between understanding ourselves as both free and subject to natural causal laws. To the extent that we consider persons in the natural world, we may view them from the standpoint of an empirical ego. To the extent that we consider persons as moral agents, we may view them from the standpoint of a 'noumenal' self – of a self 'lying behind' the natural order of the phenomenal world. This self is beyond the possibility of experience, and is therefore considered by Kant to be noumenal, or 'thing in itself'; it is not subject to the conditions of knowledge disclosed in the *First Critique*. Most importantly, this self is not subject to the category of causality, and thus escapes the principle of universal causation. With the two standpoints, Kant is able to hold both that persons are understandable as natural objects and they are free from causal determination as noumenal subjects. As noumenal subjects, Kant could allow that persons are 'free', and so responsible for their actions – that is, bound by a non-causal moral law.

One of Sartre's principal tasks in *The Transcendence of the Ego* is to reject the Kantian and (later) Husserlian transcendental ego.[14] For Kant and Husserl, there must be an I-agent (the transcendental ego) present in all conscious activity, constituting objects and structuring our experience. But Sartre emphatically disagrees and insists that 'the ego is neither formally nor materially in consciousness: it is outside, in the world. It is a being of the world, like the ego of another' (Sartre 1957: 31). Sartre insists, we have seen, that there is only one ego; there can be no duality of an underlying ego and empirical ego, as there is for Kant. There is only one self, although there are, Sartre says, two kinds of reflection, namely pre-reflective and reflective consciousness.[15]

Sartre's insistence that the ego is not in consciousness anticipates his later claim in *Being and Nothingness* that consciousness 'is not what it is', and constitutes one argument for the freedom of consciousness. Indeed, Sartre's rejection of any noumenal or transcendental ego, coupled with his acceptance of Husserl's doctrine of intentionality (all consciousness *is* consciousness *of* something), and his rejection of the Husserlian 'epoche',[16] allows him to maintain that consciousness is absolutely translucid,[17] unitary and free, and that it intends a world as standing against it. Unlike the Kantian noumenal self that is unknowable, but nonetheless presumed to be free, and so capable of moral agency in the practical employment of reason, the Sartrean *cogito* reveals no ego-agency, and although individuated, it is nonetheless pre-personal. Importantly for Sartre, the ego is in the human world (*Lebenswelt*) empirically; indeed, establishing the ego in the world, among others, is for him a necessary, although certainly not a sufficient, condition for the very possibility of moral issues.

One of the most critical points Sartre makes in *The Transcendence of the Ego* is that the relation between the 'me' and the world is one of *interdependency*. And it is precisely through the idea of the interdependency between persons and the world that Sartre understood his theory of consciousness to be able to establish a starting point for ethics:

> . . . the relation of interdependence established by this absolute consciousness between the me and the World is sufficient for the me to appear as "endangered" before the World, for the me (indirectly and through the intermediary of states) to draw the whole of its content from the World). No more is needed in the way of a philosophical foundation for an ethics and a politics which are absolutely positive. (Sartre 1970: 4–5)

Arguing that the ego is transcendent allows Sartre to view what we call our 'self', our personality and our character as the repeated outcome of the way in which we appropriate what is first given to us in the world. Thus there can be for him no privileged internal view or apprehension of myself or of my ego; my 'I' counts equally, as one 'I' among others. For Sartre, then, there can be no Kantian noumenal subject 'owning consciousness', that might – were there such a self – make choices in accordance with universal moral rules of conduct. There is only an embodied human consciousness who acts in the world and who therein makes choices and forges ideals and principles for and against others.

vi. WHAT MIGHT SARTRE MEAN OVER AGAINST KANT?

While it is true that in a number of his works Sartre uses Kantian language when discussing moral issues, he does not, I have argued, share Kant's meaning. Perhaps the most explicit example of Sartre's reference to (and seeming *endorsement of*) the universalizability principle is found in *Anti-Semite and Jew*:

For whatever the Jew says or does, and whether he has a clear or vague conception of his responsibilities, it as if all his acts were subject to a Kantian imperative, as if he had to ask himself before each act: "If all Jews acted as I am going to do, what would happen to Jewish life?" And to ask the questions he asks himself . . . he must reply, alone and unaided, by choosing himself. (Sartre 1948: 89–90)[18]

The very notion that one's reply to Sartre's hypothetical question is made 'alone' and 'unaided' in choosing oneself suggests, I believe, that Sartre is arguing *against*, not with, Kant. But if Sartre is not speaking about legislating a universal moral law for oneself in Kant's sense, what is he speaking about? We might interpret this passage in relation to similarly worded passages in some of Sartre's other works. In both *What is Literature?* and *Notebooks* Sartre speaks frequently of our being for others as a kind of 'generosity' or 'gift'. I suggest that when Sartre invokes Kant's moral language he is not speaking about legislating rules or maxims, but rather about creatively offering oneself to others in generosity or as a 'gift'. For example, in *Notebooks* Sartre states, 'So originally man is generosity, his springing up is the creation of the world . . . when he assumes himself through reflection, he makes this very creation a required and an accepted absolute . . . Everything takes place as though he had said: I choose to lose myself so that the world can exist, I choose to be nothing more than the absolute meaning of Being, I choose to be nothing so that the world can be everything . . .' (Sartre 1992: 499). It is in this sense that Sartre compares the moral act with the aesthetic, creative act in *Existentialism*: 'Instead, let us say that the moral choice is to be compared to the making of a work of art' (Sartre 1998: 42). And in *What is Literature* Sartre tells us that the final goal of art is 'to recover this world by giving it to be seen as it is, but as if it had its source in human freedom' (Sartre 1988: 57). Writing as a work of art (or any kind of human creativity, since Sartre says it doesn't really matter if it is art) is to 'both disclose the world and to offer it as a task to the generosity of the reader . . .' (Sartre 1988: 57–62). It is precisely as a task, demand, appeal and invitation that my creative act realizes itself as a kind of gift to the other so that together we may alter the world's present configuration and thereby transcend it: 'As for me who reads, if I create and keep alive an unjust world, I can not help making myself responsible for it. And the author's whole art is bent on obliging me to *create* what he *discloses*, therefore to compromise myself. So both of us bear responsibility for the universe' (1988: 57). Here we can appreciate that, contrary to Kant, authentic human choices for Sartre are contingently creative and generous in relation to a world of others, not bound by a 'moral law within'.

It might be thought that Sartre is endorsing Kant when he invokes Kant's 'city (or kingdom) of ends'. But here, too, the overlap is misleading. Because Sartre views humanity as always in the making and never as an end in itself, he does not, I believe, share Kant's meaning. In *Notebooks*, for example, he says, 'If we conceive of a perfect society (The Kantian kingdom of ends) where each person gives the other his due . . . rights are implicit . . . yet it is precisely in societies that rights can exist, because of the gap between being and what ought to be' (Sartre 1992: 137). Here Sartre's criticism of rights is similar to the eighteenth century French philosopher Jean-Jacques Rousseau's. Rousseau complains that within civil society people are everywhere unequal: 'Such was, or should have been, the origin of society and laws, which gave new fetters to the weak and new forces to the rich, irretrievably destroyed natural liberty, established forever the law of property, and of inequality, changed adroit usurpation into an irrevocable right and for the profit of a few ambitious men henceforth subjected the entire human race to labor, servitude and misery' (1987: 70). With Rousseau, Sartre observes that the declaration and existence of 'human rights' simply points to the alienation of persons in modern societies, and hence, of the impossibility of ethics today.[19] In point of fact the Kantian kingdom of ends does not exist today, and any ethical system, including Kant's and a doctrine of 'rights' that fails to acknowledge this fact, is guilty of bad faith in that such a failure ignores the present human predicament and in so ignoring it, fails to alter it. In *What is Literature?* Sartre observes,

> . . . because this universe is supported by the joint effort of our two freedoms, and because the author, with me as medium, has attempted to integrate it into the human, it must appear truly in itself . . . as being shot through and through with a freedom which has taken human freedom as its end, and if it is not really the city of ends that it ought to be, it must at least be a stage along the way; in a word it must be a becoming and it must

always be considered and presented not as a crushing mass which weighs us down, but from the point of view of its going beyond toward that city of ends. (Sartre 1988: 61–2)

Here, 'city of ends' is manifestly construed as *becoming* rather than in the Kantian sense of an 'end in itself'. When we live in a world, Sartre notes, where the other 'chooses a good that confirms' my freedom in all of my fragility, finitude and vulnerability, we are in a 'city of ends' (Sartre 1992: 500), since we have thereby conceived of a world (or situation) in which oppression and alienation are absent. Such a city of ends, though, may only be properly understood by imagining the unfolding of a future historical situation, not as an end in itself: 'In other words, by pursuing the city of ends in and through a wholly concrete goal, one marginally realizes it by proposing his work to freedoms. Hence it is the transcendence and singularity of the nearby goal that gives a value to the city of ends taken as the final goal, even though the latter gives value to the former' (Sartre 1992: 170). So despite Sartre's borrowing of Kant's language he cannot, I think, be interpreted as invoking Kant's meaning. Since his phenomenological ontology is committed to the view that our humanity is always in the making and never an end in itself it 'always realizes itself by the projection of a transcendence' (Sartre 1992: 169). It is in this sense that Sartre is critical of the self-enclosed idealism of Hegel and Comte:

However, if humanity becomes its own goal by way of individual wills, the concept falls over it again. This can be seen particularly well in Hegel where the final society can do nothing more than vegetate. It is true that he adds that the Spirit is inquietude, but he draws just one consequence from this: that there will still be wars. In an ideal society so conceived, humanity has closed in on itself. The individual man is exhausted by his relations with the whole, and the whole is exhausted by its relations with each individual. This, precisely, in one way or another, is the city of ends. It is also visible in A. Comte. The city of ends is a closed society in the Bergsonian sense of this term. (Sartre 1992: 169)

The intention behind Sartre's extending one's choice of action to all of humankind might be referred back to his claim that what distinguishes persons from everything else is that their 'existence precedes essence' (Sartre 1998: 13–16). In his view, persons can have no antecedently determined self or essence. What matters is the chosen way we exist in the world with others. And because it is true (in light of phenomenological ontology) that 'human being' has no essence, it is also true that *each* human being has no essence. I shall become what I shall now choose to become, insofar as I am this actual particular inscription in-the-world. And my particular inscription in-the-world involves others because they are affected by my choices; there is an interdependency of persons because we are in the midst of – in the presence of – others in the world. Hence the action of each of us, for better or for worse, contributes to the overall portrait of humankind.

Human universality manifestly cannot refer to some human 'essence', but to the sort of human we choose to project, to invent in a world already animated by humans. Since the ego or 'self' is outside in the world among others, persons are not closed in on themselves, but exist in a human universe. Sartre views existentialism *as a humanism* in the precise sense that persons are reminded that there is no 'lawmaker' other than themselves. Here, Sartre is in broad agreement with Kant, but he soon parts company with him in insisting that our status as 'lawmaker' is *chosen*, not imposed. Our humanity, then, is an individual adventure that takes place in the dimension of the world at large, without, however, consigning the individual to some *a priori* universal. Contrary to Kant, Sartre maintains that the morally 'universal' is not an abstract moral principle that pertains to humans solely insofar as they are rational beings, but consists of the moral principles of action which we individually choose in the endless historical and social process of making and remaking the one and only human world, in all its situational variety.

CHAPTER 8

SARTRE'S LASTING LEGACY

The idea I have never ceased to develop is that in the end you are
always responsible for what is made of you. Even if you can do
nothing else besides assume this responsibility. I believe that a man
can always make something out of what is made of him. This is
freedom . . .

> Interview with Sartre, 1970 (*New Left Review*, London)

It has been said that Existentialism, the philosophical movement
Sartre popularized in post-war Paris and most vigorously set into
motion following his 'speech', 'Existentialism is a Humanism', was
merely a reaction to the devastation of the Nazi occupation and
eventual liberation of war-torn France. The French resistance, in
which both Sartre and de Beauvoir were involved, brought fully into
view the need for sustained action, deep commitment and responsibility in a fractured world where the very meaning of humanity and
the possibility of a world in which persons could flourish, and not
simply exist, was called into question. But it would be wrong to
suppose that Existentialism was simply a reactionary movement
representing one of the most horrific chapters in human history; if
it were only that, Sartre's enduring legacy would be but a mere
footnote in the history of ideas. Freedom, the idea Sartre said he
never 'ceased to develop', remains inextricably tied to Sartre's legacy as a philosopher, novelist, playwright, cultural critic and biog-
rapher. Profoundly influenced by Descartes who, as we have seen,
transformed the capacity to doubt into a creative act, Sartre's lasting contribution is his unflinching commitment to human freedom
in a world that resists us, his insistence that we can always make

more out of what has already been made of us, and in his challenge to traditional morality that our responsibility lies not in our attachment to duty, obligation or obedience to some presumed authority, as we saw in the previous chapter, but in our own creative endeavours to carve out meaning and value in a world among others that may more closely approximate our most deeply held ideals.

While we have seen that Sartre embraces a kind of 'Socratic wisdom' that asks us to continuously question and examine our lives, he is rather distrustful of the importance both Plato and Aristotle place on the virtues as conducive to the good life. In appreciating Sartre's enduring legacy it will be helpful to note just briefly the precise sense in which he distances himself from Aristotle, in particular.

We noted that there are especially strong affinities between Sartre and Socrates with respect to the importance both philosophers place on what Socrates calls the 'examined life'. With an emphasis on 'Existence' rather than 'Reason', we saw how deeply preoccupied Sartre was with exploring the quality of our lives by asking how human and worldly happiness and wellbeing are possible. The rich affinity between Socrates and Sartre is also apparent if we view Sartrean bad faith or self-deception as an attitude that is uncritical and close-minded. Socrates, we have seen, is deeply critical of those who do not examine their own beliefs and, like Sartre, he thinks that our failure to examine our beliefs can inevitably result in an unhappy life, not only for ourselves, but for others too. Importantly, with Socrates, and Plato and Aristotle as well, Sartre is concerned to understand the psychology of human relationships; indeed, in his reflections on the possibility of an existentialist ethics, he explores the human relations of friendship and love, in particular. But for Sartre the emphasis shifts: in his view, positive human relations may occur (but, contra Heidegger, are never guaranteed) when, in authenticity we freely overcome difference or 'otherness' and achieve a 'unity in diversity' or a 'sameness' with one another, which may be expressed by actively promoting another person's freedom. For Plato and Aristotle, however, the cultivation of intellectual and moral virtues take pride of place in ethical matters and our ability to reason constitutes for them our 'essence'. Sartre, we have seen, denies that reason constitutes our essence or that our capacity to use reason to cultivate the virtues ultimately leads to the good life; rather, he compares the moral act to a work of art, emphasizing the element of creativity and invention in morality. And unlike Kant, Plato and Aristotle conceived of morality not in terms of rules or principles, but in terms of the cultivation of dispositions, traits or character; they speak, for example, about virtues and the virtuous, rather than about what is right, obligatory or a duty. Aristotle, especially, reflected on the importance of virtues to the moral life, devoting his most influential work on morality, *The Nichomachean Ethics*, to a sustained exploration of them. He argues that we ought to cultivate, through education, the proper moral virtues (courage, justice) and intellectual virtues (wisdom, prudence) that, he thought, would lead to happiness. Sartre, of course, parts company with Aristotle's views that the cultivation of the virtues are necessary to the moral life. In *Notebooks*, for example, he quips 'Good habits: they are never good, because they are habits' (Sartre 1992: 4). Here, Sartre is clearly disdainful of Aristotle's claim that one's character may become so solidly upheld by the cultivation of requisite virtues that they become habits, thereby ruling out the possibility of invention or creativity in our moral lives. Contrary to Aristotle, then, Sartre will not allow that one may simply *possess* a virtue, such as courage, for example. On his account, 'There's always a possibility for the coward not to be cowardly anymore and for the hero to stop being heroic' (Sartre 1990: 35). This would seem to be true on Aristotle's view too, yet, for him what counts ethically is that one has in fact solidly built one's moral character by practising virtuous acts. At a certain point the individual does act wholly or mainly out of habit or from a character that has been carefully and prudently cultivated; the habit, according to Aristotle, has become dominant. So it would be rare indeed, on Aristotle's account, if one were to 'act out of character' or contrary to habit. Aristotle does maintain that one may perform courageous or just acts and still not be courageous or just – having acted perhaps out of fear of reprisal. But what essentially matters for Aristotle is that one *be* courageous, and the intellectual virtue of prudence is requisite for attaining the proper moral character; prudence ensures that our actions reflect adherence to other virtues such that we will not 'act out of character'. But for Sartre, as we have seen, acting 'out of character' could be an expression of freedom, and thus could well be conducive to morality.

Importantly, Sartre would also take issue with Aristotle on another presupposition, namely, that we have a natural 'telos' or end towards which all of our actions are directed. Such a presupposition would be to set up in advance an essence of persons as essentially 'rational' or as 'naturally seeking happiness'. Both Plato and Aristotle presuppose, then, a necessary structure of human life (our rational capacity) from which they develop and demonstrate an ethical theory. Sartre's claim that existence precedes essence must rule this out because in this view persons are not definable by some characteristic, attribute or capacity, such as 'rational'; and, contrary to Aristotle, they are not naturally or essentially aiming towards some final end, except their own death. Here, Sartre is most certainly a naturalist, characterizing the human situation as the 'universal human condition' by which he means the limits that necessarily define all of us: we are united in that we all live, love, labour and die:

> Although historical situations vary, what does not vary is the necessity for persons to "exist in the world, to be at work there, to be in the midst of other people, and to be mortal there . . ." [these limits are] objective because they are to be found everywhere and are recognizable everywhere; subjective because they are lived and are nothing if man does not life them, that is, freely determine his existence with reference to them. (Sartre 1990: 38–9)

What is essential for Sartre, then, is how we live our lives; he shows little patience with otherworldly philosophies that promise life after death. *This life*, he insists, is what matters and is the only one we know and experience.

One of the most important contributions Sartre offers is his insight, first introduced in *TE*, and developed further in *BN* and *Notebooks*, that we need and depend on one another in the most basic and primary way, and that we need each other in order to live genuinely human lives. But because this primitive ontological bond is morally neutral, it is up to us to decide whether 'the ties that bind' will create the conditions for cooperation or conflict. Since there can be no prior 'we' on Sartre's account of humanity, we must forge for ourselves the conditions under which a 'we' may exist. And Sartre, we have seen, is different from much of the tradition in that he does not provide us with any absolute guidelines, rules or principles that will tell us how to create one possibility over against another. Indeed, to speak as he does of authenticity as involving the choice of creativity, the choice to *will* freedom as the foundation of the world, offers no actual guidance about the kind of world we *should* create.

Yet, given Sartre's description of the kind of beings we are, namely, persons who are situated in the world among others, and persons who must act (because not acting or refusing to act is still to act), it is not difficult to see that how the world goes depends fundamentally on us. So rather than offer a deterministic picture of persons or impute to them a fixed human nature, and then infer from this how they will or ought to behave, Sartre, we have seen, begins as Descartes did with negativity – with what we are not – and infers from this what we may become. In a word, Sartre 'defines' persons by their possibilities, rather than by a 'nature'. It is in this sense that de Beauvoir notes, '. . . unlike Kant, we do not see man as being essentially a positive will. On the contrary, he is first defined as a negativity. He is at first at a distance from himself. He can coincide with himself only by agreeing never to regain himself. There is within him a perpetual playing with the negative . . .' (de Beauvoir 1991: 33). Both de Beauvoir and Sartre, then, insist that ethics truly becomes meaningful only when there is a problem to solve – only insofar as we are at first at a distance from ourselves. Here, de Beauvoir reminds us that 'one does not offer an ethics to God' who is complete fullness and in need of nothing; the moral problem is a distinctively human problem and solicits distinctively human solutions. How do we understand what it means to be a human being? What kind of persons do we want to become? What kind of world do we want to make? Clearly, these are ethical questions of the greatest importance and urgency, especially in today's world of global instability, grinding poverty among the world's most vulnerable populations, and environmental degradation. These questions presuppose that we already live in a human world, and that the moral and non-moral values that are inscribed in the world have their source in human agency.

Notably, the great American pragmatist William James similarly argued that in order for there to be morality, there must be humanity. He claims that 'right' and 'wrong' and 'good' and 'evil' are meaningless terms apart from humanity; there is no such thing as morality in nature. James notes, 'Nothing can be good or right except so far as some consciousness feels it to be good or thinks it to be right' (James 1948: 71). Both James and Sartre are committed to a moral philosophy that consults individual human beings rather than some putative mundane or extra-mundane authority ('God' or 'Society') for answers to its questions. To be sure, this is precisely the sense in which both James and Sartre are committed to 'humanism' and defend their respective philosophy as deeply 'humanistic'.

Sartre's unique contribution is his insight that our situation in the world has been chosen and sustained by us; we have, individually and collectively, created those values and ideals that have given our world the particular meaning it has today. We have inscribed into the world those ideals and values that express our experience and understanding of what it means to be human. What kind of world have we created and sustained? If we answer this question honestly we will find that many of our choices reflected our most deeply held ideals. We will find, for example, that we have chosen to create and sustain radical disparities in wealth, both between classes living in the most developed countries and among nations. We will find that the wealthy have been content to enjoy their wealth on the backs of the world's poor. We will find that we have chosen to exploit the world's rich and beautiful resources, rather than protect them. Will we continue to sustain these conditions, or move beyond them? Sartre painfully reminds us there are no guarantees that our world will become better or worse, or that future generations will perpetuate or challenge the values we leave behind: 'Tomorrow, after my death, some men may decide to establish Fascism, and the others may be cowardly and muddled enough to let them do it. Fascism will then be the human reality, and so much the worse for us' (Sartre 1990: 31).

Because our choices are never imposed on us, it is up to us to decide the meaning of our lives in a world that is very often dangerous and uncertain. Sartre's enduring legacy is that he forcefully reminds us that we need each other in order to live truly human lives, which is to say that we need each other to collectively create the conditions under which our humanity may not only exist, but genuinely flourish.

NOTES

CHAPTER 2: SOCRATIC INSPIRATIONS

1. The reductive materialism of Paul Churchland comes most immediately to mind.

CHAPTER 3: THE IMPORTANCE OF DESCARTES

1. Sartre's view of mathematical thinking is notable here: 'Everything is stated: the object to be discovered and the method. The child who sets himself to doing a sum in accordance with the rules does not enrich the universe with a new truth. He merely repeats an operation that has been performed by a thousand others before him and that he will never be able to push beyond the same point they have reached. The attitude of the mathematician is therefore rather a striking paradox: His mind is like that of a man who walks on very narrow path where each of his steps and the very posture of his body are rigorously conditioned by the nature of the ground and the necessities of the walking, but who is nevertheless imbued with the unshakable conviction that he is performing all these acts freely. In short, if we start with mathematical intellection, how shall we reconcile the fixity and necessity of essences with freedom of judgment?'. Sartre, Jean-Paul, 'Cartesian Freedom' in *Literary and Philosophical Essays* (New York: Criterion Books, 182).

CHAPTER 4: THE HUMAN CONDITION

1. I borrow the expression 'self-announcing' from Sartre scholar, David Detmer in his book, *Sartre Explained: From Bad Faith to Authenticity* (2008, Open Court).
2. Note that the term 'must' cannot for Sartre refer to a lawful or rule-directed aspect of human conduct. It rather suggests that even in resignation or indifference we are 'making' ourselves.

3. Joseph Catalano fully develops this view in *Good Faith and Other Essays*.
4. Indeed, Sartre uses the image of a mirror in his play 'No Exit' to demonstrate the need we have of others to help us understand who we are.
5. In this passage I have substituted 'gaze' for 'regard'.
6. Joseph Catalano's *Good Faith and Other Essays* offers an excellent discussion of the relationship between bad faith, good faith and freedom in Sartre's philosophy.

CHAPTER 5: RELATIONS WITH OTHERS AND AUTHENTIC EXISTENCE

1. See especially pp. 363, 377–79 and 399–406.
2. Simone de Beauvoir discusses this form of bad faith at length in *The Second Sex*.
3. I have modified the translation to include 'transcendent' value for clarification.
4. For a more detailed exploration of this important work, see Linsenbard, G. (2000), *An Investigation of Jean-Paul Sartre's Posthumously Published Notebooks for an Ethics*. New York: The Edwin Mellon Press. I am grateful to The Edwin Mellon Press for allowing me to offer some of my views on Sartre's philosophy here, and most notably those that concern his thoughts on morality.
5. See also p. 491 for a discussion of joy accompanying the recognition of my gratuitous freedom. This reference is to the French novelist, Antoine de Saint-Exupéry, whose novels often centred on his experience as a professional pilot.
6. Sartre, J.-P. (1970), 'Intentionality: A Fundamental Idea of Husserl's Phenomenology'. *Journal of the British Society for Phenomenology*, 1, No. 2, 4–5. It should be noted that in *TE* Sartre, we saw, distances himself from Husserl insofar as he interprets him as retaining a residual transcendental ego, notwithstanding Husserl's commitment to phenomenological method. Sartre's interpretation of Husserl has been disputed among scholars, the discussion of which is too complex to pursue here.

CHAPTER 7: THE WEIGHT OF IMMANUEL KANT

1. This criticism of Kant's teachings is also found in Sartre's *Existentialism*. See Sartre (1998: 25–6, 43).
2. An example of this sort of difference in the American judicial system is the trial-court judge versus the American Supreme Court Justice. See Kant (1964: 17, 50–1).

3. Sartre is also critical of Kant's second formulation of the categorical imperative in *Existentialism and Human Emotions* (1998: 25–6).
4. See also Sartre (1992: 68, 272). Note the importance of the translation of the French word, 'realization', which here means 'making real', not 'becoming aware of'.
5. Similarly, in *BN* Sartre is critical of what he calls 'everyday morality' that is 'exclusive of ethical anguish' (Sartre 1956: 38).
6. Here the meaning of 'realizing' is certainly the pejorative, one of 'merely carrying out' some principle or standard, merely promoting or maintaining its place in the world.
7. Among them are A. R. Manser (1966: 137); M. Cranston, *Sartre*, (1962: 79ff); Mary Warnock (1965: 131–2); and Mary Midgley (1993: 105).
8. See Alisdaire MacIntyre (1957: 325–35) and Gilbert Harman (1977: 78–90). Both MacIntyre and Harman claim that because Sartre holds that different people will create different ethical principles, Sartre also holds that a person is not committed to the universalization of those principles.
9. Notably, Sander H. Lee (1985: 59–71) and R. M. Hare, Freedom and Reason (Oxford: Clarendon Press) 1963: 295–312.
10. First italics mine.
11. Thomas Anderson, for example, believes that Sartre's statements in 'The Humanism of Existentialism' are supported by 'something like an appeal to universalization', but he then notices that 'Although these suggestions have some resemblance to a Kantian notion of universalizability, note that Sartre's key word is *image*, not *rule or principle*'. Anderson concludes that Sartre's language suggests that he does not say that in choosing we adopt a rule that others who are similarly situated are to follow. See Thomas C. Anderson (1993: 69). However, in Anderson's earlier work on Sartre's ethics, he comments that Sartre's position is similar to Hare's: 'I believe the contemporary British philosopher R.M. Hare makes the same assumption by claiming that it is analytically true that reasons given in support of moral choice involve universal maxims' (see Anderson 1979: 162).
12. 'Wrongly' because commentators have ignored or misunderstood *La Transcendance de l'Ego*.
13. This is the frequently discussed dilemma Sartre describes in *Existentialism*. See especially pp. 24–5 in *Existentialism and Human Emotions* (1998).
14. As we have noted, Sartre argues that there is no reason for thinking that the 'I' gives unity to consciousness. He rejects, then, the Kantian transcendental unity of apperception as a formal, logical condition that makes it possible for the 'I think' to accompany all of my representations, and he rejects any substantial or transcendental 'I' which is

responsible for this unity of apperception. Sartre also rejects the Husserlian cogito insofar as he has interpreted Husserl as establishing the 'I think', or cogito, to be an 'absolute fact'.

15. Pre-reflectively, there is no awareness of my 'I'; there is only a direct engagement of consciousness in the world. In pre-reflective consciousness, consciousness is engrossed in this or that activity without being explicitly aware of itself; the activity of consciousness *is not known as an object*. But, Sartre maintains, consciousness is always implicitly aware of itself as free conscious activity. Hence, although there is no thetic or positional awareness of myself in the pre-reflective mode, I am always non-thetically aware of myself. When I pause and 'look at myself', my 'I' emerges and I become positionally or explicitly aware of myself.

16. In Sartre's view, we are always already necessarily in and of the world.

17. The term 'translucence' is not to be understood in a substantive sense. Translucency suggests that there is no mediation between my awareness of something and the something of which I am aware. Neither the ego nor a concept nor a perception intervenes between my awareness and that of which I am aware.

18. Also see this 'as if' proviso in *Literature and Existentialism*: 'Doubtless, the engaged writer can be mediocre; he can even be conscious of being so; but as one can not write without the intention of succeeding perfectly, the modesty which he envisages his work should not divert him from constructing it as if it were to have the greatest celebrity. He should never say to himself ' "Bah! I'll be lucky if I have three thousand readers," but rather, "What would happen if everybody read what I wrote?" ' (Sartre 1988: 23). This idea, of course, occurs most popularly in *Existentialism*: 'For every man, everything happens as if all mankind had its eyes fixed on him and were guiding itself by what he does' (Sartre 1998: 20).

19. 'Thus any Ethic which does not explicitly profess that it is *impossible today* contributes to the bamboozling and alienation of men. The ethical "problem" arises from the fact that Ethics is *for us* inevitable and at the same time impossible.' (Sartre 1963: 186).

FURTHER READING

EARLY WORKS BY SARTRE

Anti-Semite and Jew (1965), trans. George J. Becker. New York: Schocken Books [1946].

'Black Orpheus', (1988), trans. John MacCombie, in *'What is Literature?' and Other Essays*. Cambridge, MA: Harvard University Press [1943].

The Devil and the Good Lord (1960), trans. Kitty Black, in *The Devil and the Good Lord and Two Other Plays*. New York: Vintage [1951].

Dirty Hands (1955), trans. L. Abel, in *No Exit and Three Other Plays*. New York: Vintage [1948].

The Emotions: Outline of a Theory (1948), trans. Bernard Frechtman. New York: The Wisdom Library [1939].

The Imaginary: A Phenomenological Psychology of the Imagination (2004), trans. Jonathan Webber. New York: Routledge [1940].

Imagination: A Psychological Critique (1972), trans. Forest Williams. Ann Arbor: University of Michigan Press [1936].

'Introducing *Les Temps modernes*', (1988), trans. Jeffrey Mehlman, in *'What is Literature?' and Other Essays*. Cambridge, MA: Harvard University Press [1945].

'Materialism and revolution' (1962), in *Literary and Philosophical Essays*, trans. Annette Michelson. New York: Collier Books [1946].

No Exit (1955), trans. Stuart Gilbert, in *No Exit and Three Other Plays*, New York: Vintage [1944].

Saint Genet (1964), trans. Bernard Frechtman. New York: Mentor [1952].

The War Diaries of Jean-Paul Sartre (1984), trans. Quintin Hoare. New York: Pantheon [1983].

'What is Literature?' (1988), trans. Bernard Frechtman, in *'What is Literature?' and Other Essays*. Cambridge, MA: Harvard University Press [1947].

LATER WORKS BY SARTRE

Between Existentialism and Marxism (1974), trans. John Mathews. New York: William Morrow [1971].

Colonialism and Neocolonialism (2001), trans. Azzedine Haddour, Steve Brewer and Terry McWilliams. New York: Routledge [1964].

Critique of Dialectical Reason (1982), trans. Alan Sheridan-Smith. London: Verso [1960].

The Family Idiot: Gustave Flaubert 1821–1857, vols 1–4 (1971), trans. Carol Cosman. Chicago: University of Chicago Press.

Hope Now (1996), trans. Adrian van den Hoven. Chicago: University of Chicago Press [1980].

Life Situations: Essays Written and Spoken (1977), trans. Paul Auster and Lydia Davis. New York: Pantheon [1971–1975].

Sartre By Himself (1978), trans. Richard Seaver. New York: Outback Press [1976]. (This volume is the transcript of a documentary film on Sartre, also featuring Simone de Beauvoir.)

Sartre on Theater (1976), ed. Michel Contat and Michel Rybalks, trans. Frank Jellinek. New York: Pantheon [1973].

Search for a Method (1968), trans. Hazel Barnes. New York: Vintage [1957].

Truth and Existence (1992), trans. Adrian van den Hoven, ed. Ronald Aronson, Chicago: University of Chicago Press [1989].

'The writer and his language' (1973), in *Politics and Literature*, trans. J. A. Underwood and John Calder. London: Calder & Boyars [1965].

WORKS ABOUT SARTRE

Anderson, T. C. (1979), *The Foundation and Structure of Sartrean Ethics*. Lawrence, KS: The Regents Press of Kansas.

Anderson, T. C. (1993), *Sartre's Two Ethics: From Authenticity to Integral Humanity*. Chicago: Open Court.

Barnes, H. (1959), *Humanistic Existentialism: The Literature of Possibility*. Nebraska: University of Nebraska Press.

Barnes, H. (1967), *An Existentialist Ethics*. New York: Random House.

Barnes, H. (1973), *Sartre*. Philadelphia: J. B. Lippincott.

Bell, L. (1989), *Sartre's Ethics of Authenticity*. Tuscaloosa: Alabama Press.

Bernasconi, R. (2007), *How to Read Sartre Today*. New York: Norton.

Brosman, C. (1984), *Jean-Paul Sartre*. Boston: Twayne.

Busch, T. W. (1990), *The Power of Consciousness and the Force of Circumstances in Sartre's Philosophy*. Bloomington, IN: Indiana University Press.

Cannon, B. (1991), *Sartre and Psychoanalysis: An Existentialist Challenge to Clinical Metatheory*. Lawrence, KS: University Press of Kansas.

Catalano, J. S. (1980), *A Commentary on Jean-Paul Sartre's 'Being and Nothingness'*. Chicago: University of Chicago Press.

Catalano, J. S. (1996), *Good Faith and Other Essays: Perspectives on a Sartrean Ethics*. Lanham, MD: Rowman & Littlefield.

Caws, P. (1979), *Sartre*. Boston: Routledge and Kegan Paul.

Cohen-Solal, Annie, trans. Anna Cangcogni (1987), *Sartre: A Life*. New York: Pantheon.

Danto, A. (1979), *Sartre*. London: Fontana.

de Beauvoir, Simone, trans. Patrick O'brian (1991), *Adiex: A Farewell to Sartre*. New York: Pantheon.

Detmer, D. (1988), *Freedom as a Value: A Critique of the Ethical Theory of Jean-Paul Sartre*. La Salle, IL: Open Court.

Detmer, D. (2008), *Sartre Explained*. Chicago: Open Court.

Flynn, T. (1984), *Sartre and Marxist Existentialism*. Chicago: University of Chicago Press.

Gerassi, J. (1989), *Jean-Paul Sartre: Hated Conscience of His Century*. Chicago: University of Chicago Press.

Gordon, L. (1995), *Bad Faith and Antiblack Racism*. Atlantic Highlands, NJ: Humanities Press.

Heter, S. T. (2006), *Sartre's Ethics of Engagement*. New York: Continuum.

Howles, C. (1988), *Sartre: The Necessity of Freedom*. Cambridge: Cambridge University Press.

Howles, C. (ed.) (1992), *The Cambridge Companion to Sartre*. Cambridge: Cambridge University Press.

Jeanson, Francis, trans. Robert V. Stone (1980), *Sartre and the Problem of Morality*, Bloomington, IN: Indiana University Press.

King, T. M. (1974), *Sartre and the Sacred*. Chicago: University of Chicago Press.

Manser, A. (1967), *Sartre: A Philosophic Study*. New York: Oxford University Press.

Murphy, J. (ed.) (1999), *Feminist Interpretations of Jean-Paul Sartre*. University Park, PA: Pennsylvania State University Press.

Santoni, R. E. (1995), *Bad Faith, Good Faith, and Authenticity in Sartre's Early Philosophy*. Philadelphia: Temple University Press.

Santoni, R. E. (2003), *Sartre on Violence: Curiously Ambivalent*. University Park, PA: Pennsylvania State University Press.

Solomon, R. C. (1981), *Introducing the Existentialists: Imaginary Interviews with Sartre, Heidegger and Camus*. Indianapolis, IN: Hackett Publishing Company.

Van den Hoven and Andrew Leak (ed.) (2005), *Sartre Today*. New York: Berghahn Books.

Wider, K. V. (1997), *The Bodily Nature of Consciousness: Sartre and Contemporary Philosophy of Mind*. Ithaca, NY: Cornell University Press.

Wilcox, R. (1988), *Critical Essays on Jean-Paul Sartre*. Boston: G. K. Hall.

BIBLIOGRAPHY

Anderson, T. C. (1979), *The Foundations and Structure of Sartrean Ethics*. Lawrence, KS: The Regents Press of Kansas.

Anderson, T. C. (1993), *Sartre's Two Ethics: From Authenticity to Integral Humanity*. Chicago: Open Court.

Aristotle. (1990), *The Nichomachean Ethics*. Oxford: Oxford University Press.

Catalano, J. (1996), *Good Faith and Other Essays*. Lanham, MD: Rowman & Littlefield.

Cranston, M. (1962), *Sartre*. Edinburgh: Oliver & Boyd.

de Beauvoir, S. (1966), *The Prime of Life*. New York: Lancer Books.

de Beauvoir, S. (1991), *The Ethics of Ambiguity*. New York: Carol Publishing.

Detmer, D. (1988), *Freedom as a Value: A Critique of the Ethical Theory of Jean-Paul Sartre*. La Salle, IL: Open Court.

Dostoevski, F. (1960), *Notes from Underground*. New York: E. P. Dutton.

Hare, R. M. (1955), 'Universalizability', *Proceedings of the Aristotelian Society*, 55, 295–312.

Harman, G. (1977), *The Nature of Morality: An Introduction to Ethics*. Oxford: Oxford University Press.

Kant, I. (1964), *Groundwork of the Metaphysic of Morals*. New York: Harper Torchbooks.

Keefe, T. (1988), 'Sartre's L'Existentialism est un humanisme', *Critical Essays on Jean-Paul Sartre*. Boston: G. K. Hall, 84–5.

Lee, S. (1985), 'The central role of universalization in Sartrean ethics', *Philosophy and Phenomenological Research*, 46, 59–71.

Linsenbard, G. (2000), *An Investigation of Jean-Paul Sartre's Posthumously Published Notebooks for an Ethics*. Lewiston: The Edwin Mellen Press.

Linsenbard, G. (2007), 'Sartre's criticisms of Kant's moral philosophy', *Sartre Studies International*, 13, 65–85.

MacIntyre, A. (1957), 'What morality is not', *Philosophy* 32, 325–35.

Manser, A. R. (1967), *Sartre: A Philosophical Study*. London: Althone Press.

Midgley, M. (1993), *Can't We Make Moral Judgments?* New York: St. Martin's Press.

Pappas, N. (1995), *Plato and the Republic*. London: Routledge.

Rousseau, J.-J. (1987), *Basic Political Writings*. Indianapolis, IN: Hackett.

Sartre, J.-P. (1946), *Anti-Semite and Jew*. New York: Schocken Books.

Sartre, J.-P. (1955), *Literary and Philosophical Essays*. New York: Criterion Books.

Sartre, J.-P. (1956), *Being and Nothingness: An Essay in Phenomenological Ontology*. New York: Philosophical Library.

Sartre, J.-P. (1957), *The Transcendence of the Ego: An Existentialism Theory of Consciousness*. New York: Farrar, Strauss and Giroux.

Sartre, J.-P. (1963), *Saint Genet, Actor and Martyr*. New York: Mentor Books.

Sartre, J.-P. (1964), *Nausea*. New York: New Directions.

Sartre, J.-P. (1964), *The Words*. New York: George Braziller.

Sartre, J.-P. (1970), 'Intentionality: A Fundamental Idea of Husserl's Phenomenology', *Journal of the British Society for Phenomenology*, 1, (2), 4–5.

Sartre, J.-P. (1976), *No Exit and Other Plays*. New York: Vintage Books.

Sartre, J.-P. (1990), *Existentialism and Human Emotions*. New Jersey: Carol Publishing.

Sartre, J.-P. (1992), *Notebooks for an Ethics*. University of Chicago Press.

Solomon, R. C. (1981), *Introducing the Existentialists*. Indianapolis, IN: Hackett.

Tolstoy, L. (1991), *Anna Karenina*. New York: Quality Paperback Book Club.

Warnock, M. (1965), *The Philosophy of Jean-Paul Sartre*. London: Hutchinson.

INDEX